Thanks to Sue

Backpacking and Camping ━━ *in the* ━━ *Developing World*

A how-to adventure guide for travelling on your own or with a group

SCOTT GRAHAM

Wilderness Press

Berkeley

FIRST EDITION 1988
Copyright © 1988 by Scott Graham
Photographs by Kevin Graham and Scott Graham
Design by Thomas Winnett
Cover design by Tom Ridge
Cover photo by Michael Powers
Library of Congress Card Catalog Number 88-40005
International Standard Book Number 0-89997-091-5
Manufactured in the United States of America
Published by Wilderness Press
                    2440 Bancroft Way
                    Berkeley, CA 94704
                    Write for free catalog

Cover photo: Entrance to Temple of the Moon on Huayna Picchu, near Machu Picchu

Library of Congress Cataloging-in Publication Data

Graham, Scott.
    Backpacking and Camping in the Developing World / Scott Graham.
       p.   cm.
    Includes index.
    ISBN 0-89997-091-5 (pbk.) : $11.95 (est.)
    1. Camping--Developing countries. 2. Backpacking--Developing
countries.   I. Title
GV191.48.D4G73 1988
796.5'1'091724--dc19
                                            88-40005
                                             CIP

Contents

Introduction

We all have our dreams. Some dream of owning a sports car. Others dream of their own cottage in the country. Still others dream of ditching their normal life for the adventures of the open road.

My wife, Sue, and I fell into the last category. From the moment we accepted downtown Denver job offers, we dreamed of travel. Each weekend we joined the hordes of city escapees jamming Interstate 70 for a drive to the nearby backcountry. Summers we backpacked throughout the Front Range Rockies. Winters we telemark-skied to camp in a hidden valley of pristine powder tucked between two of the Front Range's goliath downhill ski areas. In our snow cave at night we talked of our escape—not just of our next weekend's trip, but of our big escape, the one we were determined to make a reality.

We thumbtacked a world map to the kitchen wall. We saved every penny. Where we should go and what we should do when we got there became our main topic of conversation. Africa, we decided. And Asia. We wanted to see what some of the rest of the world had to offer in the way of backcountry experiences.

We looked through the mass of travel books on the market. We purchased books on budget travel in the developing world and guides to backpacking routes in Africa and the Himalayas. Soon we were conversant with the vagaries of visa requirements and the severity of monsoon seasons. Our planned itinerary evolved from the half-baked

1

idea of hiking and camping our way around the world to a jaunt through North and East Africa followed by treks in the Himalayas of India and Nepal.

So we knew where we were going—or where we planned to go. But that was about it. Nowhere could we find answers to any of our basic questions on how to prepare for a trip to the developing world's backcountry. What we needed was a how-to book on backpacking in the developing world. We knew that camping in the developing world's backcountry would be far different from plunking our Coleman stove down on a picnic table in Yellowstone. But we didn't know how it would differ, nor what we should do before we left in order to survive the differences. And there was no publication that could tell us.

Eventually we gave up our search for information and went anyway. We spent 11 glorious months hiking, climbing, exploring and camping among the peoples, animals, deserts, jungles and mountains of the developing world. We learned as we went along—and often found ourselves talking about how much easier our travels would have been if we'd known before we left a fraction of what we knew by the time we got home.

We'd like to make your trip to the developing world's backcountry as enjoyable and as trouble-free as possible. That's why with Sue's help, I've written this book. We're confident it will help you a great deal, whether you're contemplating your first journey to the developing world's backcountry or you're a veteran traveler wanting to compare notes with others. The ideas, advice and suggestions in this book tell what did and did not work for Sue and me, and for others we met during and after our travels. This book contains the best advice we can give you if you're headed anywhere in the developing world's backcountry.

Ch. 1

Why Go?

Chances are you've picked up this book from a bookstore shelf, or you've stumbled upon it in your local library's travel section, or you've received it as a gift.

You've glanced at the table of contents and you've skimmed the introduction. By now you're probably thinking about some of the areas of the world you'd like to visit—the Serengeti, Macchu Picchu, the jungles of Borneo. Maybe you see yourself sitting in the bow of a dugout canoe in the middle of the wide Amazon, your paddle resting on your thighs, drops of water glinting in the moist sunlight as they fall from your paddle into the brown river.

Or maybe you're picturing the mountains of the developing world: The Andes, land of llamas and stout Indians. The wild and wet mountains of equatorial Africa, birthplace of the Nile, still so impenetrable that they harbor huge gorillas and, some say, direct descendants of the dinosaur. Or the Himalayas, grandest mountains in the world, visited by monks, traders, explorers, mountaineers, and only the most intrepid of travelers.

Maybe you've already lived or traveled overseas. Or perhaps you've never even been out of your home state. Either way, you've read of organized treks and adventures to places like the Amazon and the Himalayas. In fact, you know people who have gone on them. The trips are expensive, but you've been saving up, and are thinking of going on one of them yourself. Or maybe you suspect you could do the same sort of trip on your own. You have a lot of the necessary gear, and some expertise already.

Regardless, you've made the mental leap beyond the traditional Eurail Pass visit to Europe or the cruise-ship trip to the Caribbean. Rather, you're excited by the possibilities and are wondering about the realities of adventure travel in the developing world's backcountry. In the back of your mind, however, there may be a few lingering doubts about such a journey. Taking a trip through the developing world's backcountry—by boat, beast or backpack—isn't simple. It's far easier to stay home and read back issues of *National Geographic*. But while reading *National Geographic* is enlightening, it obviously cannot match the thrill of experiencing new sights, cultures and lifestyles for yourself. And that thrill is all the greater in the backcountry of the developing world, where the Western world's invasion of autos, planes and disposable diapers has least penetrated.

Colleges across the United States are fond of the term "experiential learning." The term fits backcountry travel in the developing world perfectly. Travel there is a tremendous experience through which you can learn while having a great time. There can be no better vacation, whether it be for a week or a year.

Fear of the Unknown

It's easy to sing the praises of journeying through the backcountry of the developing world. The hard part is working up to doing it. No matter how excited you are about the prospect of traveling in the developing world's backcountry for a month or two or three, you may still be torn between that desire and the fear of doing something that is so different from your everyday life, so unusual, that you don't really know what to expect. If so, you're not alone. Just about everyone who chooses to venture into the developing world's backcountry for the first time goes through that same battle against fear and uncertainty. Be assured, though: you may feel you don't know much about life in Africa or Asia or South America, but the folks there know a thing or two about you. As a result, they're much more prepared for your visit than you may believe them to be.

At one point during our travels, Sue and I visited Lake Turkana in northern Kenya. We prevailed upon a group of local children to take us onto the lake in two of their dugout canoes. We paddled near the local fishermen, who tossed weighted nets into the water, then hauled them back into their boats by rope to unload the fish they had caught. The centuries-old form of fishing impressed us, but not nearly as much as what we saw when we returned to shore. As we pulled the boats high on the beach, we spotted a boy of 10 or 12 standing on a log in the 110-degree heat, holding a toy guitar made of a tree branch, cotton string and a square tin can originally used as a lard container. As we walked past him, he smiled broadly and unmistakably hummed the chorus of Bruce Springsteen's song, "Born in the U.S.A.," strumming all the while on his makeshift musical instrument.

No matter where you go in the developing world, you won't be the first Westerner to visit. If you go trekking in Tibet, Marco Polo has you beat by a few hundred years. Volcano climbing in Central America? The conquistadors have been there already. Bruce Springsteen probably hasn't been to northern Kenya, but one of his fans has.

It's no longer possible to be the first. Remembering that will help you get over the fear of the unknown. The area or areas of the developing world you're thinking of visiting may be unknown to you, but you won't be unknown to those who live there. As a result, everything you need is available in the developing world. After all, more than half the world's population is surviving in the developing world, and so will you.

What Is the Developing World?

As a group, the developing countries are most often referred to as the Third World. The term relegates those countries to a less desirable position than the first or second world—the First World being the earth's capitalist, industrialized countries, or the West; the Second World being the Communist Bloc countries. Instead of the term "Third World," I'll use the term "developing world" throughout this book.

The *Encyclopedia of the Third World* defines the developing world as "the politically nonaligned and economically developing and less industrialized nations of the world." The developing countries first became a recognizable group at the end of World War II. When the United Nations was founded in 1945, nearly 30 member countries would have been classified as developing by today's standards. That number has now grown to more than 100, many of them new countries which have gained their independence in the intervening years. The countries of the developing world account for 51 percent of the world's population and 49 percent of the world's land mass. Nearly 60 percent of the people in developing nations are classified as living in poverty.

Most of the countries of the developing world lie near the equator, at least partly within the Tropic of Cancer to the north and the Tropic of Capricorn to the south. All lie south of the industrialized areas of the Northern Hemisphere. The heavy line on the map included here shows the demarcation between the industrialized north and the developing world to the south. The line separates the United States from Mexico, Europe from Africa, and Russia from southern Asia. Not included in the developing world are the Pacific nations of Japan, Australia and New Zealand.

The heavy line shows the demarcation between the industrialized north and the developing world to the south. The map is a Peters Projection, which shows the true comparative sizes of land in the Northern and the Southern hemispheres.

Ch. 2

Possibilities

Before Sue and I went to Africa, I'd never heard of the country of Malawi, nestled between lake and mountains in the southeastern part of the continent. In fact, I'd never heard of it until we arrived in Kenya, whose southern border is separated only by Tanzania from Malawi's northern border. And, I admit, I knew little more than its name when I found myself sitting beside Sue on an Air Malawi jet flying south to Lilongwe, Malawi's capital city.

Gems like Malawi lie virtually undiscovered around the world. The trick is to find them. In our case, the advice of other travelers led us to Malawi. Blind luck led us there during March, the best time of the year to visit. Temperatures were warm during the day and comfortably cool at night. The Malawians we met were unfailingly friendly and happy to have us in their country.

Our visit included a six-day backpacking trip around Mount Mulanje, the highest mountain in Malawi, a week or so of camping on the shores of Lake Malawi, the immense body of fresh water which makes up most of Malawi's eastern edge, and a camping tour of the Nyika Plateau, a high grassland of exotic scenery and animals like zebras, hyenas, antelopes and an occasional leopard.

While Sue and I camped and backpacked in Malawi, we also visited with Malawians in villages and shops and on boats and buses. We saw overpopulation and poverty everywhere. We visited with some of the white British expatriates who still live in Malawi and run many of the country's tea and banana plantations for the government. We heard tales of the repression visited upon the people of Malawi by President-for-Life Hastings Banda, tales of political prisoners and of silenced newspapers. And we spent the night at the home of a West Indian who owned a restaurant in Lilongwe. She told us of being allowed to live only in certain parts of the city and of restaurants being closed down by the government for being run too successfully by second- and third-generation Indians and other "foreigners."

In four short weeks we learned more about the problems and challenges facing Malawi than we could have learned through years of study. Learning about those problems was both enlightening and fascinating—and we had a great time experiencing Africa's backcountry at the same time. This combination of enjoyable travel and experiential learning is representative of the many journeys possible in the developing world. Our 10-week visit to Ladakh, in far northern India, is another example. Ladakh sits so far north that it is actually on the Tibetan side of the spine of the Himalayas. Today Ladakh is one of the last places on earth where Tibetan Buddhism, with its lamas and seers and oracles and monks, is still freely practiced. And it is one of the starkest, most beautiful places on earth.

During our stay in Leh, the capital of Ladakh, we saw the Ladakh that the average tourist sees. We visited the shops and the old palace. We ate in restaurants and talked with travelers from all over the Western world. We hired a jeep to visit some outlying monasteries and we spent a day at a Buddhist festival of dance, song and prayer. But it wasn't until Sue and I strapped on our packs and began climbing some of the trails up the formidable passes away from Leh that our visit really came alive. Not until we sat in a dark, stone-walled room with a Ladakhi village family and traded extra rope for barley tortillas cooked on the coals of an open fire that filled the room with smoke—not until then did we begin to see the true Ladakh. Only by journeying into Ladakh's backcountry did we get a sense of the life that Ladakhis traditionally lead, a life of planting and irrigating and harvesting, of celebrating the happiness of life and of working toward enlightenment and eventual nirvana as the Buddha's writings instruct.

Literally hundreds of areas offer tremendous possibilities for backcountry journeys in the developing world. Malawi and Ladakh are but two of them. If you want to read more about them in particular, Laurens van der Post's *Venture to the Interior* is a fascinating account of his journey to Mount Mulanje and the Nyika Plateau for the British government in 1949. And *A Journey in Ladakh,* by Andrew Harvey, is the story of the author's search for a better understanding of life—a search which brought him to Leh for an extended stay in the early 1980s. In telling his story, Harvey shares with his readers much about the lives, rituals and beliefs of the people of Ladakh.

Thousands of other explorers, travelers and adventurers have written accounts of their journeys. Some accounts make fascinating reading, some don't. Almost all, however, are packed with information that can help you decide whether you want to visit a place.

Guidebooks

If you're still wondering whether journeying through the developing world's backcountry is for you, and if so, what part of the developing world you'd like to visit, you'd do well to thumb through *The Adventurous Traveler's Guide to Treks, Outings and Expeditions.* The guide is published annually by Mountain Travel, the undisputed leader in group treks and expeditions to the backcountry of the developing world. It consists of 176 pages of tantalizing, full-color pictures of the most exotic places on earth teamed with mouth-watering descriptions of Mountain Travel's planned expeditions in the coming year.

While Mountain Travel is the Rolls-Royce of the adventure-travel industry, many competitors offering comparable trips for a lot less money have gone into business in recent years as North Americans have become increasingly interested in adventure travel. A good place to begin looking over their offerings is in the Expedition Services Directory toward the back of each month's issue of *Outside* magazine.

If you're thinking of visiting the backcountry of the developing world on your own, two publishers offer books specifically for you. Since the 1970s Australia's Lonely Planet Publications has been putting out an ever-growing and diversifying body of guidebooks aimed at those traveling the world on the cheap. The books are packed with information useful to anyone contemplating a journey to the developing world. At last count Lonely Planet had close to 40 titles in print. In addition to guides on traveling in specific countries, Lonely Planet publishes four general books which cover most of the countries of the developing world: *South America on a Shoestring, Africa on a Shoestring, West Asia on a Shoestring* and *Southeast Asia on a Shoestring.* Country by country, the guides discuss travel costs, difficulties in getting visas, length of time you're allowed to stay, and availability of public transportation. After doing your dreaming in Mountain Travel's glitzy guide, you'll be able to get down to specifics by spending some time with Lonely Planet's general guides to the areas of the developing world that interest you.

Next you may want to look over the books published by Bradt Enterprises. Bradt publishes guides to backpacking and trekking in various backcountry areas of the developing world. Among others, Bradt's titles include *Backpacking in Mexico and Central America* and *Backpackers' Africa.* Bradt's books are a great way to learn what types of backpacking journeys are possible in a given area.

Once you've settled on where you want to go generally, you can pick up any number of guidebooks on exploring the backcountry areas of specific developing countries, provided you're going to a popular area. Lonely Planet and many other publishers offer such books. For example, Lonely Planet publishes *Trekking in the Indian Himalaya* and *Bushwalking in Papua New Guinea.* If you're a mountain climber looking for peaks to conquer in the developing world, see Michael Kelsey's *Climbers and Hikers Guide to the World's Mountains,* a thick compendium listing almost every mountain on the entire planet worth climbing, with brief route descriptions of each. For the Andes and the Himalayas, there are nearly as many backpacking guides available as there are Westerners traveling to the two mountain ranges to go back-

packing. If you're planning to explore an area of the developing world's backcountry that isn't too popular, however—like
Morocco's Atlas Mountains—you'll be hard pressed to find
anything more than what is offered in Lonely Planet's general
books.

What follows is a breakdown of the backcountry travel
possibilities in the developing world. The description of each
area is brief, but enough information is included to give you a
general idea of what's there, and to enable you to narrow
down the list to what interests you. From there you may use
the Mountain Travel, Lonely Planet and Bradt guides to read
more about specific places you have in mind.

Latin America

Latin America includes Mexico, Central America and
South America. Like Africa and Asia, Latin America offers
backcountry possibilities for every taste, from some of the
world's most treacherous high-altitude climbing in the Andes
Mountains to jungle trekking through the Darien Gap, which
separates Central from South America. Public transportation
is generally a bit more modern and dependable than in Africa
or Asia, and since Spanish is widely spoken it's easier for
independent travelers to pick up enough of the language to
get themselves from point A to point B than in other areas of
the developing world, where the local language may vary from
one valley to the next. In addition, since it is nearby, getting
to Latin America is less expensive for North Americans.

Latin Americans are a fascinating mix of Indian and
Spanish cultures, with other nationalities thrown in for spice.
Their cultures are colorful mosaics throughout which the
doctrines of the Catholic Church mingle with the rituals of
Indian religions that thrived long before the arrival of the
conquistadors from Spain. Elaborate ruins offering testimony
to the advanced development of the Aztec, Mayan and Incan
cultures are scattered throughout Latin America. Today,
colorful Indian markets are evidence of those cultures' con-
tinued existence.

Much of Mexico, Latin America's northernmost country, is
criss-crossed by unmapped trails used by campesinos—the

friendly rural people of Mexico always ready to supply gringo backpackers with beans, tortillas, trail directions and home-made tequila. Few of the possibilities for specific back-country excursions in Mexico have been chronicled. Instead, Mexico is perfect for the adventurous type who likes to hop off a bus and head up whatever canyon looks interesting. For years, Carl Franz did just that. In 1981 he published a book based on his adventures, *The People's Guide to Backpacking, Boating and Camping in Mexico.* Franz is a great storyteller, and the book is an enjoyable series of tales of his Mexican adventures. Unfortunately, Franz isn't inclined to write much about the backpacking trails and hidden beaches he's found over the years, making the book pretty worthless as a guide.

My brother once enjoyed a great backcountry adventure in Mexico by taking an inexpensive excursion flight to the Yucatan Peninsula resort city of Cancun and heading off on his own from there. First he camped on the white sand beaches of Tulum, south of Cancun, then he went farther south to the fabulous ruins of Palenque deep in the jungles of southern Mexico. At Palenque he heard of a backpacking trip to a place called Agua Azul several miles to the south, where a small river becomes a series of turquoise pools flowing over limestone. He bought supplies and hiked into the area with two Swedish travelers he'd hooked up with in Palenque. After a few days of swimming and relaxation, he hiked out, jumped on a bus back to Cancun, and returned to the United States refreshed and having spent less than $100 plus the cost of his bargain flight.

Mexico's rainy and hot seasons both peak from May to September, making winter the best season for backcountry travel there.

South of Mexico, the spine of Central America offers vol-cano climbing and mountain backpacking, while its coast-lines, like those of Mexico, are for long stretches undeveloped and inviting. International buses run between most of the capital cities in Central America, while affordable flights allow travelers to hopscotch over the latest trouble spots in the region. In the countries themselves, buses trundle over rough roads to virtually every town. Like Mexico, the best time to visit Central America is during the cool, dry season from November to March.

Three Central American countries—Guatemala, Costa Rica and Panama—are of special interest to backcountry travelers. Guatemala is a rugged country of colorful Indian markets and jungle-covered volcanoes, some still active. There is boating on its swift rivers and along its quiet coastlines, and backpacking is popular in Guatemala's verdant backcountry, which hides many Mayan ruins. In particular, camping and hiking are popular in the mountains around the old colonial city of Antigua, where backpacking gear is available for rent in the winter months. A late-season trip to the area could be timed to coincide with Antigua's Holy Week observances, which include 8–10-hour processions in which townspeople carry religious floats throughout the city on streets carpeted with fresh flowers. The intricate carpets are re-woven with fresh flowers each night.

Costa Rica is Central America's most prosperous country. Because of its stable democratic government and lack of a military, it is generally considered the safest and easiest Central American country for travel by visitors. Costa Rica's backcountry is a wonderland of crystal-clear water off palm-fringed beaches and of densely overgrown volcanoes in the highlands, including Poas and Irazu near the capital city of San Jose. The many trails that snake through the highlands are popular with backpackers during the (relatively) dry winter season. It rains some 300 days a year in Costa Rica, though, so be prepared for wet weather no matter when you visit. On the Caribbean coast in the northwest is Tortugero National Park, an area of coastal rainforest dissected by canals through which visitors may float by canoe. Other national parks are found along the country's beaches and in its highlands.

For many, trekking through Panama's Darien Gap to Colombia represents the definitive backcountry adventure trip. The jungled gap forms the dividing line between Central and South America. Only through a combination of catching rides on sporadic supply boats, fording rivers, staying at jungle Indian villages and slogging for days through overgrown jungle trails can intrepid backpackers thread the Darien Gap on the southernmost part of the Central American isthmus to reach Colombia. Bradt Enterprises' *Backpacking in Mexico and Central America* provides the most detailed description of the trek available.

Unlike Central America, whose geography is fairly uniform, South America has some of everything, from Peru's Andean highlands to Brazil's Amazon jungle, from the Atacama Desert of Chile to the damp glacier-and-plain outback of Argentina's Patagonia region. Group journeys through every area of South America's backcountry are available.

The best time of the year to visit parts of South America varies greatly because the equator cuts across the northern part of the continent. The best time for visiting Colombia, Venezuela and the parts of Ecuador north of the equator is from November to April, while the best time for visiting Peru, Bolivia, Paraguay and most of Brazil, all of which lie south of the equator, is from March to September. Farther south, the climate becomes temperate, like that of most of North America. Thus, the best time for visiting Patagonia, at the south end of the continent, is during that region's warm months—November to April.

Most backcountry excursions in South America involve either the rainforests of the Amazon River Basin or the snow-covered peaks of the Andes.

Generally the only way to travel in the huge areas of virtually unexplored rainforest which still exist in many South American countries is by riverboat, although regularly scheduled flights go to some larger towns, and you may be able to catch sporadic cargo flights even deeper into the jungle.

If you're thinking of undertaking a jungle journey in South America, be prepared for some rough travel. You'll be eating what's available, drinking river water, sleeping where you can find a spot, and catching rides on whatever forms of river conveyance come along. You'll be tested by the heat, humidity and bugs. Traveling the length of one of the jungle rivers of South America (or Africa, for that matter) can take months, and unlike other travel in South America, journeys must be undertaken during the wet season, when cargo boats ply the high rivers. To many, however, a journey down the Amazon for a few months represents the perfect backcountry adventure. The scenery, wildlife and people they see and meet are worth the inconveniences.

Colombia's southern rainforest drains into the Amazon, and the Colombian town of Leticia, near the borders of Peru and Brazil, is a good starting point for those wishing to journey in the Amazon River Basin.

For those thinking of journeying in both the rainforest and the Andes during their visit to South America, Peru is a good choice. The borders of Peru encompass the heart of the Andes, so backpacking is justifiably popular in Peru. Gear can be rented both in the city of Huaraz, which sits beneath the towering Cordillera Blanca, the highest Andes in northern Peru, and in Cuzco, the mountain capital of the Inca civilization in southern Peru. The most popular trek in South America takes hikers along the ancient, paved Inca Trail for five days from Cuzco over the 13,776-foot Warmiwanusqa Pass to the magical ruins of Macchu Picchu. "The Lost City of the Andes" sits in a mountain saddle high above a bend in the Urubamba River.

A week-long trek through the jungles of the Amazon River Basin from the end of the road at Rioja in northern Peru to Moyobamba offers the adventurous a good dose of the rainforest. Local guides will show you the route and as many of the overgrown Incan ruins you'll pass along the way as you wish to see.

Far to the south, Argentina and Chile share the legendary Patagonia region, an immense area of snow-capped peaks, dark forests, lonely plains, vast glaciers and shy penguins.

Africa

Africa's more than 50 countries offer an awe-inspiring range of possible camping and backpacking journeys. For those with a genuine desire for adventure, the overland route between Cairo, Egypt, and Capetown, South Africa, has held a special allure for years. Recently, the difficulty of acquiring a visa to visit Sudan, and absent that, the increasing difficulty of traveling overland up the Nile through Sudan and

Uganda to Kenya has caused many to abandon the entire route and begin their journeys south from Nairobi, Kenya, instead.

The fact that sporadic civil wars in Sudan and Uganda have all but severed the Cairo-to-the-Cape route suggests what you must expect when planning a trip to many parts of Africa. Civil wars, political infighting and tensions between neighboring countries are commonplace in modern Africa as the continent's many newly independent countries struggle toward stability.

Kenya and Tanzania are by far the most popular African nations for Westerners to visit. While it's true that the two countries represent all that most of us think of when we picture the "real" Africa, be sure to look over a map of the entire continent before you narrow down your choices to only those two countries. For example, look to the northwest, to Morocco. Picture yourself spending a few days sipping sweet mint tea and being mesmerized by the snake charmers and acrobatic performers of Marrakech before boarding a bus for Imlil in the rugged Atlas Mountains south of the city. From Imlil you'll climb to the snowy top of 13,671-foot Mount Toubkal, the highest point in Morocco, from whose summit you can look out across the endless hot sands of the Sahara Desert.

Let your eye wander south to Zaire, land of the Zaire River (formerly the Congo) and the lush rainforests that drain into it. The possibilities for adventure—and misadventure— are mind-boggling in this land of little public transportation and nearly nonexistent roads. Backpackers have walked much of the length of the river, living off the land and its people. Other travelers have bought dugout canoes and fashioned their own river journeys. Still others enter eastern Zaire as they wander among the lush Ruwenzori Mountains, which lie on the border of Zaire and Uganda. To the south, the thickly overgrown sides of a string of volcanoes in Rwanda protect the late anthropologist Dian Fossey's beloved mountain gorillas. Picture coming face to face with an angry mama gorilla intent on protecting her young. Now that's adventure.

Then, consider the countries at the south end of the continent. No matter what you think is right or wrong in the

ongoing conflict between blacks and whites in white-ruled
South Africa, a visit there will enhance your knowledge of the
country and its people immeasurably. South Africa offers all
sorts of backcountry journeys. Many of its sprawling game
parks offer ranger-led wilderness hikes of three to five days.
The country's parks harbor most of the same animals as the
better-known parks in Kenya and Tanzania farther north,
including lions, leopards, cheetahs, elephants, giraffes and
hippos. Horseback trips into the backcountry are available, as
are hikes along undeveloped parts of the rugged South
African coastline.

From South Africa you can travel farther north by public
transportation to visit Botswana and Zimbabwe. Most of
Botswana consists of what some call the last great wilderness
on earth—the Kalahari Desert. It's possible to hire a four-
wheel drive and, if you desire, a guide for a camping trip into
the desert. Farther north the desert gives way to the
Okavango Swamps, the edges of which abound with elephants, giraffes, zebras and wildebeests. The swamps are a
labyrinth of canals and wetlands which are home to crocodiles
and hundreds of species of birds. Guided canoe-camping
trips are available in the swamps.

Zimbabwe, formerly Rhodesia, northeast of Botswana, is
said to be a model of independent black rule. A visit there
will provide you with a good contrast to the political situation you'll have seen in South Africa. Zimbabwe has an extensive national-park system with more than 250 lodges, chalets
and cottages available at reasonable prices. In some parks,
bush camps have been set up in remote areas for use by
backpackers.

Virtually every African nation is full of potential backcountry adventures. It's hard to decide what you want to do
and where to do it. Then there's the question of when. It is
impossible to generalize about what times of the year are best
for visiting various parts of Africa. Since the equator bisects
the continent almost perfectly, winter and summer are
meaningless terms except in the extreme north and south.
Instead, monsoon seasons, which vary from country to country, from one area of a country to another, and even from one
side of a mountain to another, must play a big role in your

plans. If you land in Nairobi during a normal monsoon season, for instance, you'll be lucky to get from the airport to your hotel without being washed away—and the Kenyan game parks will be quagmires of mud. It's up to you with your guidebook to figure out what time of the year will be best for you in the places you plan to go.

As in the rest of the developing world, bicycle touring is increasingly popular in Africa. Sturdy mountain bikes make it possible to see lots of backcountry, to camp off in the bush and to visit with many of the locals, who undoubtedly will be fascinated by your mode of transportation.

Of course, any solid clunker bike will do the job. Sue and I met several bicycle travelers while we were in Africa. Everyone we talked to seemed to be having a great time, even the two American women who told us of having dragged their bicycles aboard the boat that takes passengers from northern Egypt up Lake Nasser to southern Sudan. They debarked ready to ride across the Sahara, only to be halted by Sudanese border authorities. Undaunted, they snuck past the border outpost at night and headed into the desert. They followed the Sudan Railway's tracks across the heart of the Sahara for 24 days, camping each night at checkpoints built by the British every ten miles when they laid the tracks back in the days of the Empire. These days, a Sudanese family maintains each checkpoint. The families were delighted with the two crazy American women and followed their progress via telegraph.

The two made it to Khartoum, the capital of Sudan, with no problems. In fact, they told us it wasn't until they showered 24 days' worth of dust, sweat and grime from their bodies that they got their first Sahara sunburn.

Group camping safaris are the norm in Kenya and Tanzania, each of whose borders include a big chunk of the Serengeti grasslands of east-central Africa. Of the two, Tanzania is much less developed. As a result, the country is difficult to negotiate by yourself. It is not uncommon for trains leaving the capital city, Dar es Salaam, to be sold out for up to six weeks in advance. Buses are prone to break down with no means of being repaired. Sue and I met a couple in Kenya who had just arrived from Tanzania. They had had no luck buying train tickets, so they had paid an exhorbitant price in advance to take a luxury bus from Dar es Salaam straight through to Nairobi. A few hours into their journey their bus broke down. All the passengers were unceremoniously dumped on the side of the road. The bus driver began walking in the direction of Dar es Salaam; the passengers began walking toward the Kenyan border. After two days of hitching rides in the backs of trucks, the couple made it to the border, where they were able to catch a Kenyan bus to Nairobi.

Stories concerning the perils of independent travel in Tanzania are common. On the other hand, Tanzania is a great place to visit on group excursions. Organized group trips there are expensive, but groups are treated well in the country. The same is true of climbing 19,340-foot Mount Kilimanjaro, the highest point in Africa. Although the volcano is topped by glaciers, the climb's only technical aspect is dealing with the Tanzanian authorities if you wish to climb the peak on your own. The extra money you pay to be a member of a group expedition helps cut much of the red tape necessary before beginning the climb. Your group leader will be responsible for cutting the rest.

In contrast, no bureaucracy is involved in climbing 17,058-foot Mount Kenya north of Nairobi. A five-hour bus ride and a short walk take you to the Mount Kenya Youth Hostel (open to anyone) at the base of the mountain. From the hostel, it's an easy two- to three-day climb past the permanent snow line to Point Lenana, at 16,355 feet the highest point attainable without technical gear. Technical climbers may try a series of routes on rock, ice or both to reach the true summit of Mount Kenya.

Unlike Tanzania, Kenya is a fairly easy place to tour on your own. Rental cars are affordable, four-wheel drives only slightly less so. The roads in Kenya are fairly good, although giant potholes will appear without warning and in some places paved roads laid by the British have deteriorated so badly that traffic now drives on the sloping dirt shoulders of the former highways. Campgrounds are set up in Kenya's national parks for independent travelers (no such offerings exist in Tanzania). Sue and I rented a Peugeot station wagon with two Australian couples and spent 12 days going through Kenya's varied game parks, camping all the way and using the Peugeot like a Land Rover on the parks' rough roads for early morning and late afternoon drives in search of wildlife. Evenings we camped in the parks or in one of the groves of trees that sprout from the Kenyan plains. The entire 12-day trip, including food, park entry fees, gas and car rental cost the two of us $125.

Although no group trips are that affordable, some trips offered by Kenyan group-camping safari operators, who are fiercely competitive, come close, If you want to go on a group safari in East Africa but money is a concern, simply fly to Nairobi and sign up for one when you get there. By cutting out the North American middle man and all the trans-Atlantic communicating he must do on your behalf, you'll save yourself hundreds of dollars. In addition, do a little of your own leg work in Nairobi and ask around to learn which operators are legitimate. Some operators are notorious for adding hidden costs or for not delivering on all their brochures' claims. Their names and descriptions of their misdemeanors often are posted in the Nairobi Youth Hostel and on bulletin boards at Nairobi restaurants popular with travelers.

All these words on Africa touch on only a tiny fraction of the backcountry journeys possible on the continent. There are still oasis-hopping by camel in the Sahara, and snorkeling and scuba-diving in the Red Sea off Egypt's Sinai Peninsula and in the Indian Ocean off the Kenyan coast. There are surfing the huge Atlantic waves that pound the deserted shores of Morocco, and exploring the many islands off the continent's coast, including expensive Mauritius with its rugged mountains, lush forests and white-sand beaches sloping into turquoise bays. All of that and more is for you to discover.

Asia

In Asia the highest mountains on earth drop precipitously to steamy jungles and deserts give way to verdant flood-plains.

Just as the continent's geographic features give way to one another so too do the cultures and religions of its people. The Islamic religion practiced by Pakistanis in west Asia gives way to India's Hinduism, which in turn gives way to Burma's Buddhism. Farther south, Buddhism gives way to the Islamic religion once again in Malaysia and Indonesia.

Backcountry travelers in Asia are apt to learn as much about an area's religious philosophy as they area about its flora and fauna. Asia is far different, in that respect, from Africa or South America, where the former prevailing religions have been overshadowed by Christianity. Many visitors to Asia find learning about the Far East's many fascinating religions to be just as exciting as looking at Mount Everest or the Taj Mahal—and much more enlightening. Religion plays a more intimate role in the lives of rural Asians than in the lives of city dwellers, and backcountry travelers experience the personal, day-to-day relationships between people in the rural areas and their particular god or gods.

In the Himalayas travelers pass *mani* walls one after another. The walls, built of flat stones intricately carved with Buddhist prayers, may be as high as 10 feet and up to a quarter mile long. Locals carve the stones during the long, cold winters of the northern Himalayas, or during the damp monsoon seasons of the more equatorial southern Himalayas. Each mani wall is made up of thousands of mani stones painstakingly carved over hundreds of years.

Temples and monasteries are everywhere in the backcountry. Religious celebrations, feasts, fasts and dances are common, too, as rural Asians pay tribute in their many ways to the various higher beings they worship. In rural India, travelers may be lucky enough to attend one of the rare gatherings held every few years by followers of the Hindu religion. Indians by the hundreds of thousands leave their homes or their places of study with religious leaders to attend these festivals. The leaders sit in tents surrounded by their students and others interested in their particular teachings. The wisest of the leaders are generally aged and wrinkled, but their eyes burn bright with intensity and they are capable of physical feats unthinkable by yoga masters a quarter their age. The leaders hold court in their tents around the clock, sometimes offering advice and bits and pieces of philosophical wisdom, sometimes sitting relaxed and silent.

Sue and I met a British woman, Sarah, who attended one such festival in the desert of Rajasthan in northwestern India. Having lived in India for several months, she'd heard favorable comments about a particular religious leader. When she arrived, Sarah learned that he and his students were at the festival. During the next several days she spent many hours in his tent with his followers.

Sarah told us that after 18–24 hours of offering advice to troubled followers, of debating fine points of religious thought with those asking intricate questions, and of speaking quietly to those gathered in the tent, the leader's eyes would lose their intensity. The life that was so apparent in the spry leader's limbs would begin to ebb. It was then, she said, that the leader's closest disciples would convince him to separate himself from those in the tent's main room. The disciples would lead him to a private room at the rear of the tent, where, she was told, he would sink comfortably into a relaxed trance. He would appear to fall into a deep sleep, but in only a few minutes would open his eyes, which once again burned with intensity. He would then stride back into the main room of the tent, mentally refreshed and ready for another public session.

The real festival took place outside the many tents, where the devout and the curious wandered and lingered. Here Sarah saw a man with legs like the trunk of an oak tree, who had been standing continuously for more than a decade out of respect for his particular Hindu diety, spending his sleeping hours with his arms draped over a rope tied between two trees. She saw another man who looked normal in all respects save for one arm held over his head, which was shriveled almost beyond recognition. The man's arm had been healthy when, six years before, he had raised it above his head and vowed never to let it fall, as a way of showing fidelity to his god. Along with those two, thousands upon thousands of others wandered among the festival tents. Some were involved in comparable feats of sacrifice, others weren't openly involved in any, but all were gathered to study and worship and debate their religion, the single most important aspect of their lives.

Few religious gatherings in Asia are so large as those in India, but all serve to illustrate the important role that religion plays throughout the continent, where—in Muslim areas—trains and buses stop five times a day for prayers to Mecca, and where—in Buddhist areas—entire communities labor to support a monastery whose monks are not dedicated to the public good in the Western sense, but rather are dedicated to the attainment of knowledge and eventual nirvana.

The fact that the religious celebrations of Asia differ from those to which we are accustomed in the West is important to note for practical purposes as well. In most of Africa and South America, travelers can count on the week's holy day being Sunday, but not in Asia. In Muslim countries, the holy day begins at sundown Friday and lasts till sundown Saturday. Holidays and festivals about which we in the West have never heard will cause an entire country to grind to a halt—and unwary visitors will grind to a halt with it.

Some 97 percent of all Pakistanis are Muslim. As a result, the country nearly shuts down during the Islamic holy month of Ramadan, an annual time of prayer and fasting from dawn until dusk. Only after the sun goes down do businesses open and mass transportation systems begin to function normally. The month of this ritual changes according to the Islamic holy calendar, so those planning to walk through Pakistan's high, wild Karakoram Range should note when Ramadan will fall, and should adjust their plans accordingly either by being sure to visit Pakistan before or after Ramadan, or by budgeting extra time for getting around the country during the holy month.

A backpacking trip in the Karakoram is certainly a great journey to consider. The highest peak in the range is K2, second in height only to Everest. Those who wander deep enough into the Karakoram will come upon the deep valleys of the Hunza region, believed to be peopled by descendants of a lost column of the army of Alexander the Greek.

Backpacking in Pakistan's remote northern Himalayas is a good alternative to backpacking in the more popular Himalayas of Nepal, especially for those who must do their

traveling in the summer months. Pakistan's Himalayan mountains are part of a high-altitude desert like the Himalayas of
nearby Ladakh in India. Both areas are characterized by dry
weather all year, the warm summer months from May to
September (the heart of Nepal's monsoon season) being the
best time to visit.

The incredible Karakoram Highway was completed in
1978 over the 16,000-foot Khunjuerab Pass into China. It was
opened to Western tourists several years ago, instantly creating one of the most talked-about overland journeys on earth.
It is now possible to take a combination of buses and trucks
from Pakistan over the Karakoram into China and on to
Lhasa, Tibet. From Lhasa, travelers may come south across
Tibet to cross the Himalayas into Nepal, or they may journey
from Lhasa on into eastern China. As in Africa, mountain
bikes have also become a popular means of crossing the
Karakoram and exploring China and Tibet. Group treks
explore the mountains of the Karakoram Range from both the
Pakistani and the Chinese sides. Those on the Chinese side
often feature camels to carry trekkers' gear, while horses,
yaks or porters do the work on the Pakistani side of the
mountains.

Group trips are available for trekking virtually everywhere in the Himalayas, including the semi-autonomous
Indian state of Sikkim east of Nepal, the isolated Himalayan
kingdom of Bhutan east of Sikkim, and isolated mountain
areas of China. Travelers wishing to visit Bhutan may do so
only as members of an organized group, and those wishing to
visit Sikkim on their own must apply for permission to do so
six weeks in advance—from within India. The bureaucratic
morass involved in going anywhere in China is legendary; it is
even worse when attempting to travel to remote, moun-
tainous areas of the country without a guide or group.

Backpacking is popular in the Indian Himalayas, from
Islamic Kashmir in the west to the humid, green ranges in the
Hindu south and to the dry, sharp peaks of Buddhist Ladakh
in the north. Unlike in Bhutan, Sikkim and China, backpacking trips are easy to arrange in India. Trails that have
been used as supply routes for centuries climb through
passes as high as 18,000 feet to cross from one valley to

another. In some areas, valleys are so deep and have been cut off from the rest of civilization for so long that the inhabitants speak their own language. Small, independent kingdoms were once the norm throughout this area, and the palaces of the leaders of some of the kingdoms still stand on mountainsides along the routes.

Pony men are available for hire by those who do not want to carry their own gear over the steep passes, but who nevertheless wish to travel on their own. For varying rates, pony men will use their mountain ponies to carry your gear, will prepare tea for you at day's end, and, if you wish, will prepare all your meals—all for a fraction of the cost of joining an organized group trek. Backpackers and trekkers with pony men may begin their walks from a myriad of locations throughout India's mountains, but most trips are based out of the cities of Srinigar in Kashmir, Leh in Ladakh and Manali in the south. Long-distance buses go to all three cities. From them, local buses fan out farther into the mountains to trailheads, where pony men await those who wish to use their services. Trails into the southern Himalayas also leave from Dharamsala in India's southern mountains. Dharamsala is the exile home of the Dalai Lama, who escaped from Tibet three decades ago as it was being overrun by Chinese troops. Today Dharamsala is alive with the colorful handicrafts of Tibetan refugees who still look forward to the day they can return to their homeland.

Late spring and early fall are best for trekking in India's Pir Panjal and the southern mountains, which are prone to periods of rain in the summer months.

Just as Mount Everest is the highest of the Himalayas, so Nepal is the height of tourist trekking. In the more than 30 years since Westerners were first allowed to visit the backcountry of Nepal, Nepalis have taken to tourism more than any other developing country on earth. Restaurants in Kathmandu offer every type of Western cuisine, from pizza to bacon and eggs. Tea houses and hotels that once catered to the Nepalis who walked the mountain trails now cater to trekkers from the West, with hand-painted signs in English advertising hot showers and home-cooked food. Nepal may well be the perfect place for a first-time trip into the backcountry of the developing world. It is possible to trek throughout much of the country carrying only a sleeping bag, yet still eat three hot meals a day and sleep with a roof over-head each night.

The Mount Everest trek east of Kathmandu and the loop around the Annapurna massif west of Kathmandu are the two most popular treks in Nepal—and for good reason. The mountain scenery is tremendous, the local people are friendly, and the food and the hotels are decent and numerous. During the middle of the spring and fall trekking seasons, the routes are also crowded, with packed sleeping quarters in the guest houses and long waits for food. If possible, avoid the Everest and Annapurna treks during their busy seasons or carry your own tent and stove.

The rest of Asia, stretching south and east until it trails off into the island nations of Indonesia and the Philippines, varies greatly from the Himalayan countries to the north-west. Thick jungles and warm, sandy beaches characterize Thailand, Malaysia and the islands, while Kampuchea (formerly Cambodia), Laos and Vietnam are essentially off limits to Westerners.

For those wishing to look around in a jungle, southeast Asia couldn't be better. The countries of Thailand and Malaysia are modern, with air-conditioned buses and trains running in smooth contrast to the rough-and-tumble buses of the Himalayas. Trips into the two countries' jungle areas are popular and easy to arrange. Walks through the highlands of northern Thailand, which pass through areas peopled by Thailand's many colorful hill tribes, may be arranged in Chiang Mai and other northern cities. In Malaysia the many national parks open for hiking and backpacking in both the lowlands and the highlands have made the country a mecca for outdoor lovers wishing to explore the jungle. In contrast, the islands of Indonesia, particularly Borneo and Sulawesi, which straddle the equator, are little developed. Their thick, steam-bath jungles entice the hard-core backcountry adventurer.

During World War II the Japanese used Indonesian laborers to hack a narrow, 55-mile road through the heart of spider-shaped Sulawesi Island between the towns of Wotu and Poso. The road has deteriorated over the years, and today it is little more than a rough trail through the heart of the island's otherwise impenetrable jungle. Walking the trail is one of the few ways to experience the thick undergrowth, bright butterflies and gigantic insects of the equatorial Asian jungle. Jeeps that are sometimes available for hire in Wotu and Poso can take you over part of the track before they'll have to turn back and you begin walking.

Any sort of excursion into the heart of Borneo, where headhunters still roam, should provide all the adventure you could ever desire.

Ch. 3

Realities

A travel agent I know recently organized a month-long trek to the base of Mount Everest for a group of Americans. Most of the members of the group were paramedics; they were accustomed to dealing with tough situations. None, however, had been to the developing world before. Upon their arrival in Kathmandu and during the days that followed, all reported being deeply shocked by the level of poverty they saw in Nepal.

"I didn't think it would hit them that hard, considering what they do for a living," my friend told me. "It must really be something over there."

In addition to learning about all the fascinating possibilities for backpacking and camping in the developing world, it is also important to understand the realities you will encounter. Before you get on the plane to fly to Asia or Africa or Latin America, you need to know what you'll be facing in both the cities and the backcountry of the areas you'll be visiting.

Most of us have seen poverty. We've driven through (or lived in) poor sections of cities, or we've seen the run-down homes of the rural poor. None of that, however, compares with the extreme level of poverty you'll see in the developing world.

The most conspicuous poverty you'll see will certainly be in the large cities. As in the West, the cities of developing countries act as magnets. Many of the developing world's cities have become crowded downtown areas surrounded by shantytowns. Often the downtown area, while noisy and busy, has a semblance of order. But if you head away from the downtown past the heavily guarded homes of the country's very rich, you'll soon come to another city. There, perhaps millions of poverty-stricken people live in tin, wood or cardboard shacks that line narrow, dirt lanes undulating haphazardly for mile after mile in all directions. Garbage piles line the streets. Sewers are no more than open gutters. Children dressed only in torn shirts or ragged shorts, their bellies distended by malnutrition, play with toys fashioned from bits of discarded tin and wire.

The unending shantytowns are often a visitor's first view of the developing world. Since the airport is generally somewhere on the edge of the city, the shantytowns must be crossed on the way into the downtown area of hotels, travel agencies and restaurants. The road from the airport may start out as a deserted four-lane highway, but it deteriorates as it pierces the rings of poverty on the way to the center of the city. The road narrows as cinder-block buildings with rusty tin roofs close in on either side. The horns of buses, trucks and taxis mingle with loud radios and cries of food vendors standing beside charcoal braziers or vats of dark grease. People on foot crowd both sides of the roadway, which is now shared by bicyclists, donkeys pulling carts, and mad motorcyclists darting among buses, trucks and pedestrians in a vain attempt to move faster.

Most large cities of the developing world fit this description, more or less, and all suffer from poverty.

In rural areas people have space between their houses. Smoke comes from their chimneys. Cows wander by and chickens chase each other through the legs of giggling children, whose rough or nonexistent clothing seems more appropriate in the country. After the sensory shock of the city's slums, you don't immediately see the poverty that lurks in the country. It takes some time before you begin to equate the persistent coughs shared by so many, young and old alike, with tuberculosis. It takes a while before you realize that few trees still stand because most have long since been cut and burned. You begin to notice people bent double under loads of twigs no thicker than a finger, painstakingly collected miles away. As in the cities, poverty is the rule throughout the countryside of the developing world.

All visitors to the developing world come in direct contact with poverty, so it is best to be mentally prepared for it. If you're getting ready for your first visit to the developing world, anticipate having your senses jangled. Then you may not be so startled by what you see.

Crowded Buses, Long Lines

In addition to poverty, it's helpful for you as a traveler to know in advance about other aspects of the developing world that will affect your journey.

One of those is getting around on public transportation. If you'll be traveling with an organized tour group the entire time, this won't be a problem. But if you're traveling on your own for all or part of your trip, you'll most likely be using public transportation quite a bit. The incredibly high number of people who together are able to take a single train or bus ride in the developing world will astound you. Although the roof of any of these vehicles is alternately blazing hot and freezing cold or windy or rainy, it is often the preferred seating area because the interior of the vehicle, whether a ramshackle converted school bus or a vintage passenger-train car, is so packed with bodies that even breathing becomes difficult. Buses, trains, autos and fuel are in short supply in most parts of the developing world, while people and goods needing to be transported are in great supply. Hence each vehicle must carry as many people, chickens, goats, boxes and sacks of produce as possible. Public transport heading into the backcountry of the developing world is often even more crowded and less reliable than comparable transport between large cities.

The best approach, again, is to be prepared for the crowded conditions. Buy your tickets in advance if you can. Ask the advice of other travelers who have taken the ride you're going to take. Certain seats on a bus are better than others, so if possible, reserve those. When riding on public transportation, use whatever means you can to be as comfortable as possible. Keep a set of ear plugs in your pocket in case your driver has a penchant for loud music. Use your sleeping pad to sit on, or wrap your sleeping bag around your legs for warmth. Carry plenty of water and food snacks, and keep a book handy even if you can't read while the vehicle is moving. It may help to make long tea stops bearable, and it'll come in handy if the train engine breaks down or one of the bus' tires blows out. Also, remind yourself that you're in the developing world to experience it. There is no better way to do so than on public transportation. So settle back in your seat, or against the pile of luggage on the roof, smile, and help some locals with their English while you practice your Nepali or Spanish or Swahili.

If even the thought of crowded public transportation worries you, you should know that in many instances you can avoid it by spending more money. Most trains in the developing world have first-class seats available for three or four times the cost of cheap seats. Taxis are everywhere in the cities of the developing world. While they may cost fifteen to twenty times more than a city bus, they're still only a fraction of the cost of a taxi ride in the West. Walking is another way to avoid the crowded mass-transit systems in the cities while still experiencing life in the developing world. Walking across a city to get your visa extended at the ministry of tourism office may take you four hours, but it'll certainly be an eye-opening half day.

Besides crowded buses, standing in line is another constant in the cities of the developing world. If you're traveling on your own, you'll spend a lot of time in lines, whether to buy a train ticket, to change money at the bank, or to await the arrival of your bus. Spending several minutes or a couple of hours in line is much easier to handle if you're mentally prepared for it. Expect that your wait will take twice as long as you actually think it will. If you must line up to wait for a ticket window to open, bring a book for reading or a friend for conversation, and be patient. That way you won't be frustrated when the window doesn't open until two hours after it was scheduled to. When it does open and the line collapses as everyone makes a dash to be the first to the window, take a deep breath, relax, and join in the melee.

People in the developing world live in much closer proximity to one another than we do in the West. The amount of personal space they need is much smaller than that to which we are accustomed. It is common in many parts of the developing world for those waiting in line to press against each other front to back. To visitors, such closeness can be a bit disconcerting. In Nairobi a woman who had recently moved from Canada to Kenya told me she always carried knitting needles in her purse. Whenever she had to stand in a particularly tight line, she would casually allow the pointed ends of the needles to extend out the back of her purse beneath her arm. The points kept those behind from pressing tight against her.

Because of the many long lines and bureaucratic snarls in the developing world, accomplishing even a simple task can be time-consuming and tiring. During our unavoidable stays in large cities to set up our backcountry journeys, Sue and I dealt with the traffic, crowds, noise and long lines by taking them only in small doses. We decided that accomplishing one bureaucratic task each day was enough for us. And we limited ourselves to doing business in the morning—after a couple of sweltering bus rides had deposited us at government offices minutes after they had closed for lunch breaks which eventually lasted until the next day.

If you'll be traveling as a part of a group, you probably won't have to worry about this problem. But if you'll be traveling alone, be sure to budget some extra time to do your business in cities before heading for the backcountry.

Theft and How to Avoid It

You may already have heard stories about thievery in developing nations. Theft is common in the cities and on public transportation throughout the developing world. Travelers may have their handbag sliced, their pants pocket razor-bladed or their purse strings cut. In Colombia, Thailand and other countries, some visitors have even been offered drugged food or drink by seemingly friendly locals on buses or in roadside cafes. They've accepted out of politeness, only to awaken in a flea-bag hotel a day or two later with only the clothes on their backs. But most thieves in the developing world are simply opportunists. Purse slashing is rare compared to purse picking. Most people lose their wallet by unthinkingly dropping it into an open handbag or a loose pocket after making purchases, leaving themselves wide open to bump-and-pick artists. Or they turn their back on their pack in a crowded airport for just a moment too long. Or they fall asleep in a train station with their camera sitting out beside them.

Although you need not be *constantly* vigilant while you're overseas, taking a modicum of care will protect your most valuable possessions. Your passport, plane tickets, vaccination card, traveler's checks, cash and credit cards should be in your passport holder, a rectangular pouch hung around your neck on an adjustable string. One popular alternative to a passport holder is a money belt, which is a pouch belted around your waist beneath your pants or skirt. A money belt's only drawback is that access to it is difficult in public.

Before leaving your hotel room in the morning, take from the holder the spending money you'll need for the day. Put it in your pocket and don't worry about it, since it's a small amount. Hang your passport holder around your neck beneath your shirt or blouse, against your stomach, tucked into the waistband of your pants, shorts or skirt. In that position, it is impossible for a thief to grab it without stripping you—something you'd undoubtedly notice no matter how crowded the bus or the street corner.

You may find it easiest to take special care of your valuables and not worry as much about the rest of your possessions. As long as you have the items in your passport holder, you'll be all right. That's not to say it's not important to keep track of your backpack. It's just that it won't be the end of your trip if it is stolen—all gear is replaceable— whereas items like passports, vaccination cards, credit cards, airplane tickets and traveler's checks can be virtually impossible to replace.

When Sue and I traveled together, we wore our passport holders beneath our clothes anytime we were in a city, on public transportation or otherwise in a crowded situation. That got pretty uncomfortable in hot, humid conditions, but we always forced ourselves to do it. To transport the rest of our gear, we carried one large backpack and one smaller, day-and-a-half-size pack. When we traveled on public transportation, we loaded our expensive and our hard-to-replace gear like cookstove, camera, exposed film and water filter in the small pack along with books, snack food and a bottle of water. That pack we kept between our feet on the bus, plane or train, while the big pack carrying our most expendable gear, like our tent, sleeping bags and clothing, went on the roof of the bus or in the luggage compartment of the plane or above our heads on the train. On long bus journeys, we tried to keep an eye on the luggage being unloaded at each stop to be sure our pack wasn't handed into the waiting arms of an eager profiteer. In areas where this was especially likely to happen, one of us got off the bus at every stop to keep an eye on our pack.

If you'll be traveling as a couple or in a group, you may want to pair up and use the same system. If you're traveling alone, you may want to use your day pack to keep your more expensive items close to you. The trick is to protect yourself from theft without going to extremes about it.

Monsoons, Toilets and the Elusive Hot Shower

In addition to the threat of theft, there are plenty of situations that can sour your backcountry adventure in the developing world if you're not expecting them. But if you're prepared for things like misty afternoon rains and weird toilets, they'll simply be part of the spice that makes backpacking and camping in the developing world fascinating.

Since many developing countries lie near the equator, the seasons are as apt to be divided into wet and dry as into summer and winter. Monsoons are a fact of life in much of the developing world, and they must be accounted for in your plans. For example, if you're a teacher and have only summers off, you may choose to trek in the arid northern Himalayas rather than in the southern Himalayas of Nepal, which are awash in mist, mud and leeches during the summer months. Or if you like privacy, you may choose to chance the rains and take your backpacking trip on the Inca Trail in Peru just at the beginning or the end of the monsoon season, when there will be fewer people on the trail.

Indoor plumbing, if it exists, will be different from that to which you are accustomed. The toilet in your bathroom may be a two-foot-square depression in the floor draining to a hole at its rear. Rising a few inches from the depression will be two porcelain foot stands, on which you position your feet to squat and relieve yourself. Flushing the toilet will often consist of filling a bucket with water from a wall spigot and dumping it into the depression. Different from what you're accustomed to at home? Definitely. But certainly adequate.

When you're staying in a hotel or a guest house rather than camping out, hot water for your shower may be available at all times by turning on the small electric water heater in your bathroom and waiting a few minutes for it to heat up. Or you may get hot water only for a couple of hours in the morning, after the hotel proprietor has lit a fire beneath a water tank large enough to serve the hotel's guests. Or it may be available only upon special request, at which time the proprietor will dump a bucket of hot water into a tank above the hotel's only shower, providing you with enough water to wet yourself, soap up and rinse. Or hot showers may not be available at all.

Sue and I timed our trek along the popular trail to the base of Mount Everest to coincide with the tail end of Nepal's monsoon season, to avoid the crowds of tourists who visit the area during the dry season. At one of the houses we asked our host about the possibility of taking a hot shower, as the sign above the front door advertised. Certainly, she said. But her eyes said perhaps not.

She put water on to heat and had us sit near the fire in the kitchen, then left without a word. Outside, we heard her calling for her son. We watched from the window as he left the group of children with whom he'd been playing and ran to his mother. She bent over him, talking earnestly and pointing at a shed about twice the size of an outhouse that sat behind the main house. We noticed that a length of plastic hose ran from the house to the roof of the shed. Having given her orders, the woman headed back into the house. She shooed us away from the window as soon as she returned, but not before we saw her young son open the door to the shed to release six or eight goats. By the time the water was warm, the boy had cleaned out most of the straw and droppings from the goats' monsoon-season barn. Sue and I took turns showering in the wooden-floored shed, hollering to the woman when we needed more smoke-smelling water funneled to us from the kitchen via the plastic hose to the shower head in the shed's ceiling.

Haggling

Prices for goods and services you buy along a popular trail—like meals, lodging and hot showers—are generally set. That's not true for handicrafts and gift items you buy on your journey, nor for produce bought at markets. For those things, haggling is the rule. Haggling over the price of goods is a way of life in most of the developing world. If you want to pay anywhere near market value for goods you buy in open markets and shops, you'll have to learn to play the game. Treating it that way—as a game—makes it easier to do.

Although you may be uncomfortable with the notion of bargaining with a salesperson over the price of an item you wish to buy, you should remember that the salesperson assumes you will haggle since that is what is done in his country—and he sets his opening price accordingly. You need to know the market value of the item you wish to buy before you try to buy it. Ask other travelers what they paid for various items you may wish to buy, from a kilogram of bananas to a hand-woven sweater. Armed with that information, find the particular bunch of bananas or the sweater you want, then begin bargaining with the salesperson. If you want to buy expensive items at market value, always be prepared to walk away from a shop without making a purchase, no matter how much you may like an item. In fact, walking away from a shop a few paces often leads the salesperson to offer you a price close to the market value of the item you're interested in. If the salesperson lets you walk away, you'll know he's given you his lowest offer. You can go back anytime to buy the item at that price.

As a Westerner, you'll be considered rich no matter how tight a budget you may be on. Therefore, it is expected that you will pay slightly more for goods and services than locals. You may see it as acceptable to pay a little more than locals do for the goods you buy, but you probably won't want to pay the opening price for those goods, since the first price quoted by salespeople to Westerners is often two to four times an item's market value. So, though you may feel awkward about it, you'll probably end up haggling.

Ch. 4

Basics

If you're a first-time traveler to the developing world, you've most likely got plenty of concerns. You may be wondering how much your trip will cost, how you should carry your money, and how to get more when your cash runs out. Perhaps you're wondering what vaccinations you need, or whether cheap flights are available to where you're going.

Fortunately, many North Americans travel overseas— more than 10 million each year by one count. They've worked out the answers to all these questions and more. All you have to do is determine which of the answers best suit your needs.

Cost

Travel in most developing countries is remarkably affordable. Travel in the backcountry of the developing world is an even better value. A huge breakfast in Kathmandu, for example, won't cost you more than 75 cents. On the trail, breakfast in a guest house will be less than half that.

In Nairobi, a night in a good, clean hotel room will cost you $5 to $7 for a single, $8 to $10 for a double. Cheaper but often dirtier hotel rooms may be found for half as much. In other Kenyan cities, comfortable hotel rooms will range from $4 to $6 for a double.

Of course, it's possible to spend much more on food and lodging no matter where you are. The Nairobi Hilton averages more than $100 a room. Like all Hiltons around the world, the snazzy hotels of worldwide chains like the Bangkok Sheraton and the Cairo Oberoi all charge Western prices for the Western amenities they provide. Their food is just as Western as the food served in the Kansas City Hilton, and just as expensive.

Public transportation is also inexpensive in the developing world. The 8–15-hour bus ride (depending on the number of times your bus breaks down) over countless ridges of the Himalayas from Kathmandu to Jiri, the trailhead for the trek to Mount Everest, costs $2. A first-class train ticket good for the length of the Egyptian Nile is $8.

All these prices are representative of the costs of traveling in most of the developing world, but a few countries are considerably more expensive. They include Argentina, Brazil, Chile, Malaysia, Ghana, Nigeria, Gabon and Congo in West Africa. If you'll be traveling in any of these countries, your food, lodging and transportation costs will be higher.

For our trip Sue and I each budgeted $10 per day. We were able to stay within that range easily. Our $20 per diem covered food, lodging, snacks, small gifts and ground transportation. Flights and expensive gift items we budgeted separately. While we didn't stay in any Hiltons, we avoided flophouses too. Most of our hotel rooms were higher quality and thus more expensive than those used by the many shoestring travelers we met, who were stretching their funds as far as they could. On the other hand, the fact that we camped out and mostly cooked our own food in the backcountry saved us a lot of money. If you'll be spending much of your time in the backcountry, you'll probably be able to stay within a similar budget, assuming the dollar remains fairly stable against foreign currencies. Your costs will be higher if you'll be traveling alone, and you should budget accordingly. If you'll be traveling with a group, you need only enough money above the cost of the tour for gifts and miscellaneous expenses.

Money

Now that you have a rough idea of how much your trip is going to cost, how do you go about carrying all that money?

If you don't like credit cards, now's the time to change

your thinking. If at all possible, get an American Express card before you leave on your trip, and also bring a few personal checks. Start with $1000 or so in American Express traveler's checks. When that begins to run low, simply stop in at the nearest American Express office (there's at least one in every large city in the world), flash your card and write a check for the amount (up to $1,000) you want in additional American dollar traveler's checks. It's that easy.

You'll exchange your traveler's checks for local currency at banks or hotels or on the black market. Banks will take a percentage as their commission for exchanging the money; hotels will take a larger cut. American Express checks are the most widely accepted, but most types of traveler's checks will do if you exchange them legally.

Developing countries with a government-mandated rate of exchange that does not reflect the true market value of the country's currency often have a flourishing black market through which you can exchange your dollars at a better rate than at a bank. Cash will get you the best rate, American Express will also be accepted, and any other type of traveler's check most likely will not. While you'll pay no commission when exchanging money on the black market, you'll run the risk of having your money stolen by the black marketeer with whom you're doing business, and you'll run the lesser risk of being arrested for your activities. More on the physical and philosophical risks of dealing on the black market appears in Chapter 6.

If your trip will be short, you'll probably be able to bring all the money you'll need with you in the form of traveler's checks. It's still a good idea to have an American Express or a Visa card with you for emergencies—and for that Persian rug you simply must have. Regardless of how many checks you're carrying, leave a list of their numbers with someone at home and, separate from your checks, keep a list of your check numbers and the places and dates that you cashed them. If you're traveling with someone else, simply trade lists with your partner. That way, on the fateful day you lose your checks, you'll know exactly how many were lost and what numbers they were. Should you or your partner lose your separate list, you can always call home for the numbers. Be sure to carry a few $50 and $20 traveler's checks in addition to larger denominations so you can exchange them for a small amount of cash when that's all you need.

If you can't carry a credit card, your next best option is to take all the money you'll need with you in traveler's checks. If you'll be gone a long time, that'll be quite a wad of checks, so be especially careful about keeping track of their numbers as you cash them. If possible, avoid having money wired to you in the developing world. Not only is it difficult to arrange and time-consuming, it can also be very expensive.

If you enter a developing country by air, you'll be able to exchange money at the airport, but often you'll receive less local currency per dollar at airport branch banks than at downtown banks. Ask ahead. If that's the case, just exchange enough at the airport to tide you over until you can get to a bank in town.

Save all your receipts from money-changing transactions. If you have local currency left over when you're ready to leave a country, you'll need the receipts in order to change it back into dollars or some other currency you can use elsewhere. (Most currencies of developing countries are so unstable they are worthless outside that country's borders.) Plan ahead so that you finish your stay in a country with as little of that country's currency left as possible, since you lose a percentage of your money each time you exchange it.

In addition to your traveler's checks, always carry anywhere from $100 to $300 in cash. American dollars are by far the best to carry, but any stable Western currency will do the job. That cash will serve you well in emergencies.

During our travels in Africa, Sue and I parted, she to work in Sudan, I to fly on to Kenya. In my Lonely Planet guide, *Africa on a Shoestring,* I had read of the interesting city of Juba on the upper Nile in southern Sudan. I planned to lay over in Juba for the week between Khartoum-Juba flights and Juba-Nairobi flights.

Only two other Westerners boarded the Sudan Air jet with me in Khartoum. After we were airborne, I left my seat and crouched in the aisle of the half-full plane to talk to them. The two men were British. Both looked to be in their forties.

One was skinny and pallid, the other had paunch enough for his friend and me too.

"So, you're headed for Juba?" I asked.

"Unfortunately," replied the skinny one.

"Why unfortunately?"

"Because of the war, of course."

"War?"

"Yes. They've been keeping it pretty quiet in Khartoum, but apparently the SPLA has been acting up again. They've got Juba surrounded and the road's been cut off, or some such."

I knew government troops had been skirmishing with the Sudanese People's Liberation Army in the south, but I had no idea anything serious was happening.

"Then why are you going to Juba?" I asked.

"We work there. We're used to this sort of thing, you see. And why are you going?"

I swallowed.

"Well," I said, "I thought, well, I thought I'd like to—see the place."

They both looked at me blankly.

"Oh," said the skinny one.

We circled the mud-walled, thatch-roofed town of Juba once before landing. Below me I saw a crowd of people pushing to get into the airport's only building, a ramshackle, tin-roofed affair slung low in the heat. Although the air conditioner had cooled the interior of the plane considerably, I began to sweat.

The wet, muggy air of the upper Nile combined with the superheated air rolling off the Sahara slapped me in the face as I climbed off the plane. Hundreds of people were pressed against the barbed-wire fence that surrounded the runway and ran up against both sides of the faded terminal building. All were trying to get in the building's outer door.

I walked with the British gentlemen to where our bags were being dumped from the plane onto the tarmac. I cleared my throat once, wondering if I could trust my voice.

"All those people are trying to get back to Khartoum, eh?" I asked shakily.

"I daresay they're trying to escape, the lucky devils," said the skinny one. "But the ones who make it will escape for good. This plane goes on to Nairobi."

My heart skipped a beat. I grabbed my pack and knifed through the thick air to the terminal. Inside was bedlam. A jostling, screaming, crying crowd proffered tickets, passports and money to the beleaguered Sudan Air employees at the counter before them.

I stepped behind the counter and tapped the most senior-looking employee on the shoulder. His dark hair was speckled with gray, and when he turned to me he looked calm despite the turmoil around him.

"Onward ticket?" I asked. "Nairobi?" I motioned at the plane.

"Yes," he said in English. "Since you are a foreigner, you must pay in dollars—$175."

"No problem," I said. "I've got American Express."

"No checks. Dollars."

"What?"

"Only cash."

Now I really started to sweat. "All I have are checks," I said.

"I am sorry but the Sudan Air does not accept traveler's checks."

"In Khartoum they do."

"Yes. In Khartoum, that is so."

"Is there anyone else I can talk to?" By now my voice had reached a frequency above that of the other cries filling the building. The room quieted as more and more eyes focused on me.

"No. I am head man," he said. "There is no one else."

"Do you realize what this means?" I shrieked at him. "I have no dollars. There is a war out there so I can get no dollars. They say the road is severed. I'll be trapped in Juba for the rest of my life!"

"I think in a week you will find the money," said the man. He put on his best travel-agent smile. "And Juba is not such a bad place."

"But look at all these people trying to leave! I am told I cannot even go beyond the edge of the town!"

His smile tightened.

"Yes, this is true. But . . ."

There was an ominous silence after he stopped talking.

"I am sorry," he said. He turned back to the counter. Immediately, my sideshow over, the cries of everyone else again filled the room.

I stumbled off, mopping the sweat from my face. I'd not gone three steps when someone touched my elbow.

"What's the problem? What's the matter?"

Despite being nearly bald, with red hairs pasted across the top of his white head, the man speaking couldn't have been more than 35. His voice identified him as a New Englander.

"I need $175. Cash."

He pulled an envelope from beneath his shirt and began counting twenties from it.

"How much?"

"$175. No. No, $160. I've got $15 cash."

I was sputtering in my nervous relief. The man smiled and handed me the money. "We'll settle up on the plane," he said before ducking out the door to the runway.

I approached the head ticket agent and handed him the money. He filled out my plane ticket with a flourish. I grabbed my pack and followed the last of the passengers to the plane. Inside I spotted my red-headed saviour and signed over eight $20 traveler's checks to him. He turned out to be a worker for a Mennonite Church-funded relief organization. Save the two Britishers who had just arrived, he was one of the last Westerners to leave Juba.

As soon as I reached Nairobi, I went to a bank to get some American currency. The bank employee refused to give me any for my traveler's checks. I concocted a lie about owing $200 to an American who was leaving Kenya for the U.S. the next day. At that point I didn't care about lying, I just wanted some Western currency. The employee bought my story and handed over the dollars—but only after taking a 10 percent bite for the bank.

Neither Sue nor I needed such a large amount of Western currency again during our travels, but throughout the remainder we used bits of it here and there when banks were closed unexpectedly or when we wished to buy film or other items from other travelers about to return to the West. Having some American currency with you will serve you the same way—and will bail you out of a Juba-type emergency, should you find yourself trapped in one.

Mail

If you're planning to travel for long, you'll want to receive mail. That's another good reason for being an American Express customer. All American Express offices hold mail for up to 30 days as part of the services they offer customers holding an American Express card or using American Express traveler's checks. In so doing, American Express has created the only reliable way to receive mail overseas—and they've created all kinds of traveler's-check and credit-card business for themselves in the process.

The only alternative is the "poste restante" (mail holding) service offered haphazardly by many post offices in developing countries. How well the service works depends on whether the particular post offices you select are run with any sense of organization, whether postal workers think something of value might be contained in envelopes addressed to you, and whether workers who look through the waiting mail for you know how to spell your name.

American Express claims it will hold only flat mail for its customers, but small packages containing items such as film are generally held—if they get through the country's postal system. Too often, postal workers in the developing world steal small packages coming from the West. Sue and I received only one of five small parcels sent to us overseas. As far as we know, however, we did receive every piece of our flat mail.

Packages mailed out of developing countries to the West generally are safe. Crooked postal workers are interested in Western goods coming into the country, not in handicrafts and other goods made in their country going to the West. Everyone Sue and I met who mailed packages to themselves in the West from the developing world received them—eventually. (Sea mail can take up to six months; air mail might take only a month or two, but it will cost up to five times as much as sea mail.) We heard of problems only from those who bought expensive items like carpets and paid shop owners extra to have their purchases shipped to their homes. The owners did nothing of the sort, obviously pocketing the cash and keeping their goods.

Your best bet is to carry everything home yourself. Your next best bet is to mail items yourself at as large a post office as you can find—preferably the main post office in a capital city. Doing so may mean a day's worth of standing in a line and filling out senseless forms, but at least by the end of the day you'll know the items for which you so diligently shopped are on their way home. If you're having a shop owner mail something expensive for you, watch while your package is wrapped and accompany it to the post office; otherwise, be prepared to receive a cheap imitation of what you actually bought—or nothing at all.

Passports

Passports—especially U.S. and Canadian—are worth lots of money to thieves. Keep yours on your person beneath your clothes at all times. If you do lose it or have it stolen, you'll be able to replace it through your country's embassy, but it won't be easy.

In the United States passports cost $42 and are good for 10 years. Allow up to two months for processing before the summer tourist season; allow a month any other time. Application for passports may be made through a post office, the office of a county clerk, or the office of the U.S. State Department in large cities. You'll need proof of citizenship (your birth certificate or a certified copy, or a previous passport), identification (a driver's license and a credit card), two 2″ by 2″ full-face photos in color or black and white with a plain background, and your money.

Visas and Other Entry Requirements

A visa is a stamp in your passport giving you permission to visit a country. Visas are also the cause of unending hassles at foreign embassies around the world.

Visa requirements vary from country to country, from day to day, from border post to border post and from official to official. In many cases, visas may be obtained at the border or the airport upon your arrival. If not, you'll need to get them from embassies in your country before you leave or from embassies in other countries before you arrive at the country you need a visa for. Be sure to find out whether you must have a visa in advance before flying into a country or arriving at its border. If you don't have the visa you're supposed to have, you'll be shipped out on the next plane or you'll be turned back at the border.

The length of time your visa allows you to stay in a country generally is 30–90 days. Some countries have no time limit, others allow much shorter stays. Burma, for instance, allows visitors to stay for a maximum of seven days. Other countries have special 24- or 48-hour visas for airline passengers waiting for connecting flights. Costs for visas vary, too, from no fee to $20 or more. One official at a Venezuelan Embassy in Colombia requires visa applicants to get an expensive syphilis test at a clinic down the road before he'll issue them visas. Whether the clinic is operated by the official's brother is open to speculation. See the guidebooks to the country or countries you'll be visiting for more specific information.

If you'll be visiting only one country that requires a visa, you may consider applying for it before you leave by mailing your passport, the required fee and any additional forms or photos to the country's embassy in your home country. Be sure to do so well in advance of your trip.

If you'll be visiting several countries, don't count on obtaining all your visas before you leave home. Many visas must be used within a certain time of their issuance—generally within three months. Also, after receiving passports in the mail with correct payments, foreign embassies have been known to delay sending passports back with visas stamped in them. They have even been known to fail to return passports at all.

In planning your trip itinerary, give some thought to avoiding visa hassles and to accommodating restrictions. Study the visa information sections of your guidebooks to figure out what will work best for you. Many Asian cities, for example, have foreign embassies that are difficult to deal with. Bangkok, on the other hand, has many efficient embassies representing other Asian countries. The same visa that might take two weeks of struggle to obtain elsewhere could be yours overnight in Bangkok. If you're planning a trip to several southeast Asian countries, you may want to start in Bangkok for that very reason.

In addition, for no apparent reason, the cost of a visa for a given country may be 10 times as much in one country as in another. Planning ahead to take advantage of cheaper costs may be worthwhile too. Also, bring two dozen passport-size photos along with you if you'll be visiting many countries, since virtually every visa application must be accompanied by two to four photos. Officials of developing countries often require you to pay for your visa in American dollars or another Western currency. This provides a steady flow of hard currency for the country, but it can be problematic for you if you haven't enough dollars or if you haven't the correct denominations of bills, since embassy officials may refuse to give you change.

Even after you have your required visa and arrive at the border or airport of the country you wish to visit, you may still face problems. Some countries will refuse entry if your passport shows proof that you've visited a particular country previously. For instance, most Arabic countries won't allow entry to holders of passports showing any hint of travel to Israel (Egypt being a notable exception). Most black-ruled African countries won't allow entry to those whose passports show that they have been to South Africa. Zimbabwe and Botswana, which depend on South Africa for imports and exports, are exceptions.

Both Israel and South Africa will put your entry and exit stamps on a piece of paper which you can throw away when you leave. But this won't do you any good if you leave either country overland, since the border-post stamp you receive in the country you enter proves that you left Israel or South Africa to enter that country at that point. Suspicious immigration officials half a continent away will spot such details and will turn you back despite your pleas for leniency.

Some developing countries that have a black market for exchanging money require you to exchange $100, $200 or even $250 at the official rate when you enter the country. Other countries may require you to have a return or an onward plane ticket before you can enter the country, despite the fact that you'd planned to leave the country overland. In some countries, that requirement is used selectively to hassle people acting belligerently and people dressed shabbily. In other countries the requirement is applied to every foreigner wishing to enter. Still other countries—or even particular border officials—will require you to show that you have at least $500 or so in cash or traveler's checks before you'll be allowed to enter.

Leaving a country can also present problems. Some countries require exit visas, which can take days to obtain. Countries that don't require you to change money upon arrival may, instead, require proof of your having changed a certain minimum amount of money legally before you'll be allowed to leave. That's true in Tanzania, where the government-mandated rate of exchange is so artificially high that a bottle of Coca-Cola costs several dollars. As a result, visitors have resorted to changing money on the black market, which is very open, and have endeavored to fool the border officials when they leave by doing things like exchanging $10 at the official rate and then adding a zero to their receipt to make it look like they've exchanged $100.

But altogether, you shouldn't have any serious problems if you study the various visa and entry requirements as stated in Lonely Planet and other guidebooks to the developing countries on your itinerary, know what countries have embassies where, who charges what, and what requirements must be fulfilled where—and use all that information when figuring out your itinerary.

Vaccinations

Only a few vaccinations are required for entry into developing countries. However, you shouldn't leave home without getting several others. Be sure to have all your vaccinations noted on the yellow International Certificate of

Vaccination you should receive with your first shot. Carry the certificate with your passport, and leave a photocopy at home in case your original is lost.

Large cities in North America have vaccination centers, which should have all the vaccines you need at reasonable cost. Some private hospitals have started international clinics that offer vaccinations as well as medical advice to the growing number of North Americans headed overseas. Plan ahead for your vaccinations, since some require follow-up shots.

Cholera is one of the vaccines immigration officials may require before they'll let you enter their country—despite the fact that the shot does little good. The vaccine is only 40 percent effective at best, and is good for only six months.

Yellow fever is the other vaccine commonly required by the many countries whose people suffer from the disease or which fear its introduction—that means all of Central and South America and Africa. The yellow-fever vaccine is good for 10 years.

Meningitis flares up occasionally in isolated areas, as it did a few years ago in Nepal. When it does, authorities of the affected country may require that you be vaccinated against it before they'll let you enter. Don't worry about getting the vaccine unless there has been an actual flare-up reported in an area you plan to visit, since meningitis is rare and the vaccine hard to come by.

The **typhoid** vaccine isn't required, but it is essential for anyone going into remote areas of the world. It is even recommended by some for those going into remote areas of the United States. The typhoid vaccine is given in two doses about two or three weeks apart. It gives most folks a pretty sore arm, but that beats heck out of having the disease. The vaccine is good for one to three years depending on the strength of your dose.

As a way to boost your immune system to help it fight off **hepatitis,** an injection of two to five cc (depending upon your body weight and the length of the dose's effectiveness) of gamma globulin as close to the date of your departure as possible is highly recommended. Gamma globulin's effectiveness is still being debated, but anything is worthwhile which helps you fend off one of the most common diseases in the developing world, and one that can have devastating and lasting effects. The shot is good for only three to six months, but gamma globulin can be found at many vaccination centers in the developing world—and boosters are certainly a good idea if you'll be overstaying your first shot's effectiveness.

A **diphtheria-tetanus** booster shot is generally needed every eight to ten years or if you suffer a deep laceration or a puncture wound. Since you'll probably end up with small cuts and scrapes while in the backcountry of the developing world, and may have a hard time keeping them clean as they heal, it's a good idea to get a booster before you leave.

Be sure you've been vaccinated against **polio** at some point in your life. Polio is under control in the West, but it is a very real problem in much of the developing world. Check with your doctor or vaccination center—a booster is often recommended.

Smallpox, on the other hand, has been eradicated, and the vaccine for it is not longer required—or available. The **typhus** vaccine is generally not recommended. Pills must be taken to help fend off **malaria,** which is prevalent in many areas of the developing world. The types of pills available are covered in Ch. 10.

Remember that all vaccines only help your body fight off disease; they don't guarantee that you won't contract something. In addition to getting the correct vaccinations before you leave, you must do what you can to protect yourself on your journey. That means avoiding unsanitary eating utensils; staying as clean as possible; keeping all cuts and scrapes clean and disinfected; avoiding being bitten by insects; and avoiding water and food that you suspect—especially salads, dairy products and street food fried in grease whose age may be suspect. All of these precautions are covered in detail in Chs. 8, 9 and 10 on water, health and food.

Other Documents

In addition to your passport and your vaccination record, you may wish to carry two other documents.

The International Youth Hostel Federation oversees hostels throughout the world. IYHF hostels are great places to stay and to meet other travelers. They usually include separate dormitory-style sleeping quarters for males and females, a communal kitchen, and a lounge area often boasting a library and a notebook full of suggestions from former visitors. They're generally clean and, despite the name, there is no age limit.

Holders of an IYHF card, which costs $20 per year, stay at the hostels at the lowest rate, generally $1 to $3 per night in the developing world, while those who don't have a card must pay slightly more. If you'll be traveling extensively in a country like Argentina, where hotel lodging is comparatively expensive and hostels are many, buying an IYHF card may pay off. If most of your time will be spent camping in the backcountry and/or traveling in countries that don't have extensive hostel systems, you'll probably save money by paying the higher price at the few hostels you run across.

Don't let the word "hostel" fool you. Many inexpensive lodging facilities in the developing world use the term as part of their name. While some are clean, affordable hotels, many have cockroaches and prostitutes, including some government-run hostels.

Once upon a time, an International Student Identification Card was an indispensable companion for any traveler who looked younger than 40. Many countries offered discounts as high as 50 or even 60 percent to holders of the card on anything from plane tickets to museum admissions. It didn't take long for a flourishing trade in counterfeit student cards to arise. Eventually, governments began to catch on to the fact that almost every traveler carried one of the cards. As a result, while the card is still quite useful in some countries, many have done away with the card discounts altogether and offer discounts only to people younger than a certain age, usually 24 or 26, as shown on their passport. If you have been a bonafide full-time student in the last nine months and plan to visit several countries on your journey, it's probably worth your while to get one of the cards. Contact your school to find out how to do so. If you'll be traveling to only one or two countries, or you'll be traveling with a group, the card probably won't pay for itself.

Photography

You're probably planning to take lots of pictures on your journey, so you'll be able to impress everyone back home with photos of your exploits. If so, the following suggestions may help assure that you get the most from the time you spend shooting photographs while you're traveling.

First, know your equipment before you leave. This simply repeats what everyone else says, but it's worth saying. Because trips to the developing world are expensive and time-consuming, they are rare occasions for most of us. Don't risk your photos of what may be a once-in-a-lifetime trip by buying new equipment and not learning to use it before you leave. Buy equipment far enough in advance to run through more than one practice roll.

All X-ray machines in airports around the world have signs saying they won't harm film. I don't believe them. When I fly, I carry my film in a clear plastic bag separate from my carry-on luggage. I hand the bag to the attendant to look over while I step through the metal detector, then collect it on the other side. No attendant has ever refused to hand-check my film, and I've never created a scene by asking to have it done.

I allow my camera to go on through the X-ray machine with its roll of film. Attendants are less happy to hand-check cameras, since they're bulky enough to conceal bombs and what not. That's fine with me. I don't want any bombs on my plane either. I figure if the one roll in the camera gets ruined, I can live with the loss. I just don't want my whole stash of film ruined by a berserk X-ray machine.

As for what equipment to carry, despite a wide variety of choices, the selections made by most travelers are fairly standard. If you're not overly interested in photography, but do want some shots for memory's sake, either of two choices will suffice. Pocket 110 cameras are fine for snapshots of people you meet along the way, but for scenery photos their lack of quality hurts. The new family of pocket 35-mm cameras are a better choice—and they're also more expensive. These cameras do an admirable job of capturing both people and scenery, they're simple to use, and they're lightweight. The larger 35-mm, single-lens reflex (SLR) cameras are by far the most popular among travelers. They're heavier and bulkier than pocket 35-mm cameras, but the exceptional pictures they're able to produce make them worth their weight to most photography hobbyists. For SLRs, separate wide-angle, 50-mm (normal), and telephoto lenses provide crisper images than a single zoom lens of comparable quality that covers all three ranges, but three lenses are also much heavier than one.

Film speed is a personal choice. I sacrifice quality for simplicity. I'm content to carry 200-ASA, which is a fairly fast film. It works in most low-light situations without requiring me to set up a tripod to hold my camera steady. On the other hand, the colors I get with 200-speed film are not nearly so vibrant as I would get if I shot 64- or 100-speed prints or slides.

No matter what type of film you choose, try to bring all you'll need. Film is available in the developing world, but even if it is not out of date, you can't tell whether it has been stored at the proper temperature. It'll also be more expensive than in North America, and your selection will be limited. The exceptions to all that are the large, modern cities of southeast Asia, where the camera craze is nearly as strong as in Japan. Film prices in southeast Asian cities are competitive with the West, quality is generally not suspect, and equipment prices are often far lower than back home.

For processing your slide film, you can use Kodak mailers. These handy envelopes can be purchased in the U.S. Their cost covers the processing charge for one roll of Kodak slide film. When you finish a roll of film, all you have to do is seal it in the sturdy envelope, attach the correct postage and send it off to the nearest Kodak processing center. Once processed, your slides will be sent to the address you indicate on the envelope. The mailers are great because they enable you to get your film out of your hands as soon as it is shot, minimizing the chances of its being lost, stolen or destroyed during the rest of your trip. Your only risk is that the film will be lost in the mail. If it is, at least you'll lose only one roll, rather than the many you could lose near the end of your journey if you kept all your exposed film with you.

Flights

If you'll be traveling on your own at all, you'll be considering various hotels and restaurants, trying to find the best quality for the lowest price. You'll spend a lot of time doing this, and by being choosy you'll save a steady stream of money.

Studying your international flight possibilities the same way may pay off a great deal more. If you're headed for the Andes, for example, searching long enough to find an inexpensive fare to San Jose, Costa Rica, then flying on to Peru from there instead of taking a far more expensive direct flight could save you several hundred dollars.

There are two reasons a hop-scotch flight may be the best way for you to get to your destination. First, it is less expensive to fly from a developing country than from the U.S. to just about any destination. Second, some U.S. cities, London, Amsterdam, Nairobi and several Asian cities have what are known as "bucket shops." Bucket shops are travel agencies that sell inexpensive tickets for airlines that choose to dump excess tickets on the market, often for less than half the lowest regular fare, rather than fly their planes half empty.

This practice occurs in the U.S., but not to the extent that it does in other parts of the world. Check the small air-fare advertisements in newspaper travel sections to find agencies in New York, Los Angeles, San Francisco and Miami that may have low-priced tickets available to various destinations from time to time. The practice is openly accepted in London, where many bucket shops do business. It is venerated in southeast Asia, whose cities are favored by those searching for inexpensive flights. If you'll be traveling through southeast Asia during any part of your journey, try to arrive there at the end of a one-way ticket. You'll be glad you did, as you wander past the many competitive travel agencies advertising their latest low fares on chalkboards leaned against their front windows.

One note: Most of the airlines that use bucket shops to sell their excess tickets are not the world's classiest. If you buy a bucket-shop ticket, you'll most likely be flying an airline like Pakistan International Airways, Philippine Air or

Internal-frame packs like the one being carried by this hiker in the highlands of Ecuador keep the weight of your gear low and close to your back.

The best known section of the Inca Trail leads trekkers to Macchu Picchu, "The Lost City of the Andes."

Tanzania's Mount Kilimanjaro towers above a pair of gazelles.

Responsible travel means respecting the natural, social and spiritual environ-
ments of the places you visit. Here Buddhist monks in the Ladakh region of
India's northern Himalayas prepare to paint the two-story-tall Buddha they're
constructing in the Lingshet monastery.

This musical panhandler on the streets of Cuzco, Peru, provides a welcome counterpoint to the cries of children for candy, money or pens that often greet visitors to developing countries.

If all is quiet as the date of your departure approaches, it'll most likely stay quiet during your visit. Like this newsboy in Lima, Peru, you'll need to have only a nodding acquaintance with the local headlines during your travels.

Two Swedish backpackers take a break near the top of a pass in Bolivia.

If you carry a tent, be prepared. Your mode of shelter is bound to provoke visits from curious locals of all ages, like this young boy on the trail to Mount Everest in Nepal.

Pony men in the Indian Himalayas will use their mountain ponies to carry your gear, will prepare tea for you at day's end, and, if you wish, will prepare your meals, too—all for a fraction of the cost of joining an organized group trek.

When the crowded Lake Nasser ferry pictured here anchors at night during its three-day run between Egypt and Sudan, the boat's toilets discharge directly into the same water that is pumped aboard to replenish its drinking-water supply. The ferry's obvious water problem is but a microcosm of the inadequate sewage and water-treatment systems that create tainted water supplies throughout the developing world.

"Decadent" is the only way to describe some of the "campgrounds" Western travelers are treated to in countries like Malawi, shown here, where the members of an expatriates-only country club welcome Western campers and backpackers—especially those who agree to sit in for a few hands of bridge in the evening.

Aeroflot, rather than a classy airline like Thai Air or British Airways. You'll be subject to the poorer service and higher incidence of delays and cancellations that characterize lower-budget airlines.

If your destination is somewhere in Asia, another possibility you can explore is that of buying a round-the-world ticket. For one price, this ticket allows you to work your way around the world in a fairly straight line within a specified length of time, usually six months or, for a higher price, a year. You must select your layover points in advance, and must stick to them. Two airlines usually team up to offer the ticket. Your travel agent can help you figure out whether such a ticket might work for you, and if so, which pair of airlines would best enable you to reach the places you want to visit. Africa and Latin America do not lie in the flight paths of most of the world's airlines, which ply the skies of the Northern Hemisphere for the most part. So if you want to head south to visit either as part of a round-the-world ticket, you must pay more.

Thanks to increasing numbers of international travelers hunting good deals, cost cutting is becoming more and more common among international airlines. Your job is to find out who's offering what. First, go to the library and read the Sunday travel sections of certain cities' major newspapers. If you're in the east and are headed for South America, look at the Miami papers. If you're in the west, check the Houston and Los Angeles papers in addition to Miami. Headed for southeast Asia? Try the Los Angeles, San Francisco, Seattle and Vancouver papers. West Asia? Either coast may work for you. Africa? New York.

As you continue your search, find a travel agent who has dealt with international flights and see what he or she can find for you. In addition, specific guidebooks will give you more information on the many possibilities for getting to your destination.

There are other options available for finding inexpensive international flights. One which seems to be discussed wherever travelers gather is that of becoming a temporary courier: a briefcase is handcuffed to your wrist to be delivered somewhere overseas. When you take on such a burden, your flight is supposed to be free or nearly so. I've heard of this happening, but I've never met anyone who has actually done it. I did meet an American man in Bangkok who looked much older than his 30 years who told me of being propositioned to smuggle something—he was never told what—from Thailand to Hong Kong. He was to receive a free flight plus a good deal of cash when he delivered the suitcase to an address in Hong Kong. Upon his arrival, however, he was nabbed by two Hong Kong immigration officials, who hustled him and his suitcase into a car and drove to a desolate section of the city. There they beat him senseless, took the suitcase and left him in an alley. He awoke fearing for his life at the hands of those to whom he was to have delivered the suitcase, and spent his last dollars to get out of Hong Kong as quickly as he could.

When you're looking for inexpensive flights, be persistent but not foolish.

Ch. 5

The People

While we were in Ladakh, Sue and I backpacked through the Markha Valley beneath the high and wild Stok mountain range. The scenery was beautiful, but our timing was disastrous. During our 11-day trek, the high-altitude desert area around us received an onslaught of rain worse than anything the locals could remember.

The rains began as we headed up the valley. By the time we were halfway along, many of the valley's bridges had been washed out and miles of the trail had disappeared. Getting from one village to the next was a mad scramble up muddy slopes to avoid crossing the roaring Markha River at places where the trail had been washed away. But despite our best efforts, we were forced to ford the river over and over again. Each time we came to a place where the river tore into the side of a vertical rock face, we had no choice but to find the widest possible spot and make a wet crossing by swinging pendulum-style to the far side of the river at the end of our 50-foot length of rope, fighting for balance in the churning, waist-deep water.

Finally, we left the valley behind and topped a 17,000-foot pass to return to the Indus Valley and Leh, the capital of Ladakh. On our tenth day we were only a few miles up a side canyon from the Indus River and the busy road that follows the river's course back to the city. We were exhausted, as was our food supply, but the next day we would return to civilization. As it got dark, we pitched our tent on point of land just off the trail, which led back and forth across the side canyon's narrow creek. It had stopped raining, and we fell asleep beneath starry skies. Not until we'd slept for several hours did the rain begin again. It came in a rush, with a forewarning wind howling down from the pass, followed by splatters of rain pellets, then the familiar drone of steady drops against our tent. By the next morning the narrow creek was a muddy torrent far worse than the wide Markha had been. It gnawed at the walls of the tight canyon and pushed hard at the point of rocky land on which our tent stood.

Although the rain had slackened to a drizzle, there was no way to cross the still-deepening creek. Downstream from our camp we worked our way up a cliff as far as seemed practical. From our perch we could see the trail continuing down the far side of the creek until it disappeared around a bend. We inched our way off the cliff and huddled in our rain jackets.

Later in the day the rain ended, but the creek remained a torrent. Then came a flash of movement on the cliff above. Working her way steadily down the cliff we'd climbed earlier was a young Ladakhi woman. She used one of the Ladakhis' sturdy, waist-high walking sticks to balance herself against the rock wall's uphill side. In the barren desert land of Ladakh, the sticks are considered a valuable possession. Behind the woman followed a nimble old man with a huge cloth pack slung over one shoulder. Not until the woman came close did we see that on her back she carried a baby wrapped in blankets. The woman smiled broadly as she stopped before us. After our greetings, we learned through hand gestures that the three had come from the Indus Valley. They assured us that no crossings of the creek were necessary for us to reach the main valley.

Noting the doubt in our eyes, the woman left her child with the older man and led us back up the cliff. From the point we'd reached earlier, she pointed out a route off the cliff's far side and on down the canyon. Using her stick for support, she moved smoothly back down the rock face to our camp. Sue and I followed slowly. At camp, the woman swung the child to her back and turned to leave, brushing aside our thanks. Then, as the old man watched with twinkling eyes, she turned and held out her walking stick to us. We insisted that we could not accept it, but she merely smiled and persevered. Finally we accepted her gift, and with a wave she and the old man headed up the canyon.

Sue and I traded off using the stick for balance as, sure enough, we worked our way out of the canyon without another crossing.

Encounters like ours with the Ladakhi woman are common in the developing world. Bob, a traveler from Georgia, told us of leaving a stuff sack filled with knickknacks like his sewing kit, Swiss Army knife and extra flashlight batteries on a bus in Kenya. Three days later his bus driver spotted him as he walked by the bus depot. Bob told us of the driver's wide smile as he returned the full stuff sack to him.

Those are the sort of stories you'll return home with from your journey to the backcountry of the developing world. Yes, you'll remember the towering peaks, the forbidding deserts and the tropical rainforests, but more often you'll remember with greater clarity your encounters with the people of the developing world.

Many Westerners plan visits to the developing world's backcountry with visions of pristine wilderness in mind. At the outset of their journeys, however, they quickly learn that pristine wilderness no longer exists in the developing world except in the harshest deserts, the thickest jungles and the highest mountains. All the other land is inhabited by fascinating, friendly, warm-hearted people—but by people nonetheless.

If you desire only to commune with nature in the developing world's backcountry, be forewarned. The only way to do so is to pass through backcountry areas inhabited by locals to reach the few parts of the developing world still relatively uninhabited. Luckily, most of the locals in the developing world's backcountry are a pleasure to be around. They are like the woman who recognized how weary Sue and I were, and who gave us her walking stick as her unspoken bit of encouragement to us. They are happy, giving human beings living lives of quiet strength, often in situations of extreme poverty.

No matter how much privacy you may want, rarely on your

trip to the developing world's backcountry will you be out of sight of the locals. For the most part, that continuous interaction with the locals is welcome and refreshing. Greeting a Bolivian woman in her bowler hat as she smoothly glides past you on a narrow trail high in the Andes is inspirational, and it is a pleasure to see that children are children—playful, carefree and laughing—no matter where they live.

This continuous interaction can sometimes get difficult. Everyone is curious to some extent. You are curious, or you wouldn't be considering travel to foreign lands. The people of the developing world are curious about you as well. After all, with your colorful backpack, your high-tech gear and your snazzy sunglasses, you make quite a sight.

Privacy? Who Needs Privacy?

In North America we're accustomed to the high level of privacy that comes with affluence—single-family homes, private cars and large tracts of wilderness land into which we can escape to hike and camp without being disturbed. The situation is much different in the developing world. Generally, people there must live close to one another. The familiarity that comes from that closeness carries over to visitors, and they are not afraid to openly study newcomers, especially weird ones who cook on fancy stoves and pump their water through strange devices before they drink it.

On your journey you'll become accustomed to having children tag along with you, and to having locals whom you approach on the trail come to a halt and stand scrutinizing you intently until you exchange greetings and pass by. You'll grow used to having an audience watch you set up your tent and cook your dinner each time you camp near a village. Despite knowing in advance that as a traveler in the developing world you will have attention centered on you, you may still find that attention difficult to handle at times. If so, the following suggestions may help you find some privacy when necessary.

In the city: If you find yourself the continuous target of honking taxi drivers, shouting vendors and imploring beggars in a big city, treat yourself to a nice meal at a restaurant in a fancy Western hotel. You won't be hustled for your money there—but the prices on the menu will force you to spend it. And while you're doing so, you'll be treated with the indifference you desire and the hotel's patrons expect.

On public transportation: Again, treat yourself. Over time, despite your best efforts to rationalize the situation, the curious crowds on buses and trains may get to you. You may sit in a packed, sweltering train compartment with twenty sets of eyes staring at you for hours. Despite the interludes when students practice conversing in English with you, several of those rides in a row may still be hard to bear. If so, splurge periodically on a first-class ticket and ride in private, air-conditioned comfort to your destination.

On the trail: Even while trekking through the beautiful countryside of the developing world, the feeling of being nothing more than an object of attention may get to you. To combat it, you may choose to carry a tent, even when lodging in guest houses is available. In the large, dormitory-style sleeping rooms and communal dining rooms of the guest houses that line the developing world's most popular trekking routes, there is little privacy. In comparison, the combination of eating and visiting with locals and other travelers in the guest houses, then retiring to your tent to sleep, will most likely afford you that small amount of privacy you need.

On the other hand, if you'll be traveling with an organized group, your guide should provide you with all the insulation from the locals you want. In fact, that's one of the drawbacks to organized group travel—your guide acts as the intermediary with the locals, and you don't get much contact with them. The solution is simple—break off on your own a bit. Hang back from the rest of the group during the day and greet all the locals you meet along the way. If your meals are being prepared by porters, skip dinner one evening when you're camped near a village, wander into town and inquire about the possibility of getting a bite to eat. As long as the food you manage to track down is freshly cooked, you shouldn't have any worries. Even if you don't manage to find anything, the interaction you'll create between yourself and the people of the village will be fascinating for both sides.

Whether you're traveling alone or in a group, there are

several other ways you can increase interaction with the people.

For starters, learn some of the language. You don't have to learn a lot, just the formal greeting phrases and a few basics like "yes" and "no." You'll be amazed by the goodwill you'll create and the respect you'll be treated with just for stuttering out the few words you've managed to learn in the locals' language. If you really want to break away on your own and talk with the locals, carry a pocket book on the language of the area you're visiting—and don't be embarrassed to use it.

For the rest, your English will most likely serve you quite well. English is the international language. Not everyone knows it, but it will get you by in most places. In general, you'll be able to find someone who speaks a smattering of English no matter how deep into the backcountry you wander. And if you don't, you'll learn very quickly how well you can communicate using hand gestures.

Another way to stimulate interaction with the native people begins with reading about them before you go. Start with the most specific guidebooks you can buy. Then go further: pay a visit to your nearest library. You'll be amazed at all the novels and nonfiction books you'll find about the area you plan to visit. Work your way through a few of them. When you're overseas, the knowledge you'll have gained will help you understand all that is happening around you.

While you're reading about the area you'll be visiting, be sure to take careful note of the area's predominant religion, since it will play a big role in the lives of many of the people you'll be meeting. If you're aware of their religion and how it affects their lives, you'll be able to treat their customs with the respect that comes from knowledge. In the Himalayas, for example, trails constantly split to go around Buddhist mani walls made of carved prayer stones. It is correct to pass with a wall on your right, and to pray as you walk by. It would be rude to pass with a wall on your left, or to speak to others as they walked by a wall.

It is also important to learn and follow the dress code of the area you'll be visiting. In Malawi, that's easy—the dress code is specified by law there. It is illegal for women to wear pants or shorts; only dresses or skirts below the knee are allowed. For men, long, unkempt hair is reason enough to be turned away at the border. Elsewhere, dress codes are much more subtle, but important nonetheless. In many parts of the developing world, Western women are permitted to wear pants or shorts even though local women wear only long dresses or skirts. While wearing pants or shorts wouldn't be impolite, wearing a long skirt will make for quick acceptance by the local women. Generally, wearing bikini tops and short shorts is considered impolite everywhere except on the beach, where it may be perfectly acceptable for women to be topless. Again, consult your guidebooks and ask the advice of those who have been where you're headed. Once you're there, trust your own judgment based on observation. Showing respect for the customs of the people whose land you are visiting will go a long way toward creating good relations and good experiences with them.

Finally, there is one international symbol that everyone from the youngest child to the oldest curmudgeon responds to—a smile.

Ch. 6

Wars, Bureaucracy and Other Impediments to a Good Trip

While the bureaucratic snarls that are part of traveling in many developing countries are frustrating, an untimely war with assorted bombs, grenade launchers and machine-gun fire is much worse. Being trapped in a hotel by a 24-hour curfew during a coup attempt would put a damper on anybody's vacation. For the most part, however, as a traveler you're immune to trouble caused by intra- or inter-country squabbles in the developing world.

Actually, a bit of alertness on your part when you're making your travel plans will allow you to avoid trouble spots in the developing world. The amount of international news available in the West is more than enough to let you determine whether your proposed visit to a certain country or region of the developing world is safe. If all is quiet as your departure date approaches, it'll most likely stay quiet during your visit. Political trouble usually bubbles for a while before boiling over. Keep a close eye on the international news pages in your newspaper. If you're American, you may wish to call the U.S. State Department to check the list of countries it recommends avoiding, as well as the list of countries Americans are forbidden to enter.

Once you're in the developing world, the amount of information available to you shrinks considerably. When you're overseas and you need information about the safety of a particular country or region about which no news is available, your next best sources are your country's foreign embassies and other travelers. But remember that whereas almost any sign of political trouble will cause an embassy to recommend against visiting a particular country or area, many travelers tend to think that all is safe as long as no bullets are flying directly at them. By their nature, travelers are adventurous. As a rule, that's fine, but be aware of that fact when you ask for advice on the safety of an area you're considering visiting.

Sri Lanka is a perfect example. The island nation off the southern tip of India has been torn by civil war since the mid-1980s. This wonderland of undeveloped beaches and verdant jungles has not been a safe place to visit the last few years, but that hasn't kept travelers from going to the island. When we were in New Delhi, Sue and I met a New Zealander, Johnny, who had just come from six weeks of traveling along the Sri Lankan coast.

"It's wonderful," Johnny told us. "The people are friendly, the food is great, and since there are hardly any tourists, the Sri Lankans are so desperate for business that everything is virtually free."

He went into a long description of succulent fruit, delicious seafood stews and inexpensive jeep rentals. Although at the time the strife in Sri Lanka was being covered extensively by the international press, Johnny didn't mention a word about the war until we brought it up.

"Oh yes, that," he said. "Well, it's certainly made things quiet as far as tourists go. But I never heard of any fighting or anything while I was there."

Unlike Johnny, your best bet is to heed stories you read of wars and unrest in places you wish to visit, whether in North American papers or in those overseas. Beyond what you read, your best guide is common sense, something that is lacking in a surprising number of overseas travelers like Johnny.

Bureaucracy

While not nearly as dangerous as running into an unexpected war, bureaucracy is much more of a daily problem in the developing world. Generally, you'll run into bureaucracy whenever you do anything that involves the government of a developing country, from mailing a package to getting a visa. Like bureaucracy anywhere, only patience and knowledge can help you deal with it.

Learn as much as you can about the bureaucratic idiosyncrasies of the places you'll visit by reading the available guidebooks before you leave on your journey. Upon your arrival, talk to other travelers to find out what schemes and what preparations will cut down the time required to deal with the government.

If you learn that visas for the country you'll be visiting are available both upon your arrival and in advance at the country's foreign embassies, purchase your visa when you arrive. You'll save yourself at least two trips to a foreign embassy in an obscure suburb of some capital city whose staff may or may not be efficient and your visa will be issued to you on the spot at the border or the airport upon your arrival. Even if "on the spot" means a two- or three-hour wait, or if obtaining a visa upon arrival costs more, it'll still be worth it.

Once you're in the developing world, what should be a simple procedure can turn into a nightmare if you don't know what to expect before you visit the government office responsible for whatever permit, visa or license you need. Obtaining a trekking permit in Nepal is a good example. The address of the government agency that issues the permits will be in your guidebook, but rather than go straight to the office, you should do some asking around first. From other travelers, you might learn that the office's hours have changed from those listed in your book, or learn the best time to arrive at the office to avoid long lines, or learn what information will be required for you to get your permit. You may be told that you need to know exactly where you're going trekking and for how long, or that you'll need to show receipts for having legally changed—in advance—at least $5 per day from the day you arrived in Nepal through the last day of your permit's effectiveness.

Armed with all that information, you'll have legally exchanged the necessary money before going to the permit office. You'll arrive at the office a half hour before it opens and stand in line with a few others trying to beat the crowds that will descend on the office later in the day. You'll have your exchange receipts plus the required two passport photos and money for the permits. When the door to the main room opens, you'll know to grab a trekking permit form from a stack on a shelf and fill it out quickly. You'll know which is the correct window for independent trekkers, despite the lack of any signs in the room, and you'll join the line there as soon as you complete your form. When it's your turn at the window, the official will check your form, note that you have all the necessary information, take your money, and give you your permit.

As you leave, others will be madly trying to figure out what trekking route to apply for on their forms as the lines in front of the windows rapidly lengthen. Others will have filled out their forms and waited through a line only to learn they must go to a bank and change money legally. For you, learning all that you could beforehand and arriving at the permit office fully prepared will have paid off.

Learn all that you can from other travelers about any activities you must undertake—bureaucratic or otherwise. Learn the location of train and bus stations in advance so you won't get lost on the way to an important departure. Know how early you should board the train or bus to be sure of your seat—even if you have a reserved-seat ticket. That's *the best way* to deal with bureaucracy in the developing world: even if you don't understand a bit of it, figure out what works and do it.

Bribery

Although petty bribery is a way of life for many in the developing world, you probably won't have to resort to bribes unless you choose to.

Before leaving on our trip, Sue and I met with one of Sue's former teachers, who had spent the previous three summers as a volunteer doctor in Senegal, Africa. Police roadblocks were common in Senegal then, while ballpoint pens were scarce. To negotiate his way through the roadblocks, Sue's teacher handed out pens to police officials along his route.

We left with a pack of Bic pens in our gear and kept them handy at border crossings. However, while pens were scarce and hence valuable in remote Senegal, we quickly learned that nothing short of dollar bills would have served as bribes in the more Westernized countries we visited.

Beyond petty bribery, larger-scale bribery is considered part of travel in the developing world by a few unscrupulous Westerners.

In Nepal, for example, the Lukla airstrip high in the Himalayas near Mt. Everest becomes a tourist bottleneck twice a year. During the spring and fall trekking seasons, thousands of visitors are ferried in and out of Lukla in 12-passenger, twin-prop planes operated by Royal Nepal Airlines. When the weather is good, the planes fly in and out very frequently. When bad weather sets in, however, no planes dare attempt to thread their way up the deep Khumbu Valley to land on Lukla's steep runway, which ends at the lip of a precipice.

When the weather lifts, there may be as many as 500 trekkers from the West filling Lukla's guest houses and camped in the surrounding meadows, all intent on catching the first plane to Kathmandu. In theory, seats are allocated on a first-come, first-served basis. In reality, those with the most cash win, if they so choose.

One German trekker spent five days in Lukla before the weather lifted. Since he'd been waiting as long as anyone, he expected to be on one of the first flights out. Instead, when he looked at the list posted in the shed which serves as the

Royal Nepal Airlines terminal in Lukla, he saw that his name was nowhere near the top. A while later he saw an American heading across the grassy runway to board one of the planes. The German had seen the American arrive only the day before.

Enraged, the German sprinted across the runway, tackled the American at the bottom step of the plane, and began wrestling with him. Nepalese police officers broke the two apart and dragged the German away for questioning. And the American? After many profuse apologies from the Lukla representative for Royal Nepal Airlines, he boarded the plane and flew to Kathmandu. He'd paid his bribe; he got preferential treatment.

The Black Market

It is common practice for travelers intent on making a little extra money to buy a liter of Johnny Walker Red Label and a carton of Marlboro cigarettes at airport duty-free shops when they fly into a country where Western liquor and cigarettes are heavily taxed or in short supply. International law allows the importation of a liter of liquor and a carton of cigarettes per person. Those items can then be sold at their inflated street prices. For liquor, that might be as high as three times a bottle's original cost—even higher in countries where hard liquor is frowned upon or outlawed.

It is also possible to exchange Western currency and even traveler's checks on the street at better rates than you would receive at a bank. Indeed, in some countries, black-market money exchanges are as common as bank exchanges—and far simpler, too.

Be sure to consider all the consequences of your actions before deciding to deal on the black market. First, learn what the penalty is for being caught playing the black market in the country you're visiting. In countries where the black market is open and is seemingly used by everyone, the penalty for being caught using it may be several years in prison. Even if no one you talk to has ever heard of anyone being prosecuted for dealing on the black market, you have to ask yourself if you want to take the chance of being the first tourist to be faced with fighting such a harsh penalty in a foreign court system. Also, ask yourself what damage your black market dealings may do to the country you're visiting. It is clear, for example, that any tobacco or alcohol you sell on the black market will contribute to the poor health of those in the developing world. And in some cases, Western currency obtained on the black market is used to finance drug-smuggling operations or the slaughter of rare animals for their tusks or pelts.

Ch. 7
Responsible Travel

McDonald's has reached Bangkok. AT&T is in China. And Dr. Scholl's arch supports are for sale in Cairo. As multinational corporations battle for business and territory in what is their last sales frontier, they're changing ways of life for people in the developing world. Sweatshirts featuring Western rock bands are popular in Thailand; throughout Africa Mercedes Benz automobiles are the preferred form of transport; and around the developing world Western blue jeans are *haute couture.* Western culture is coming to the developing world, and the developing world is welcoming it with open arms.

As a representative of Western culture, you'll be welcomed with open arms too. As such, you'll be affecting the lives of everyone you meet—especially in the backcountry, where, with your backpack, boots and bright clothing, you'll be a living example of all the West has to offer.

Recently, American financier Malcolm Forbes decided to travel up the Amazon River. He invited several aristocrats from Europe to join him and away they all went—first in Forbes' personal jumbo jet, then in a yacht complete with a helicopter, speedboat and staff in starched white. Forbes and his guests shot clay pigeons off the back of the yacht, and participated in a nighttime alligator hunt. To me, that's the antithesis of responsible travel in the backcountry of the developing world. But just how do you go about traveling responsibly?

To travel responsibly requires that you realize that the actions you take during your stay in the developing world will continue to affect the lives of the locals and their environment long after you have gone. During your journey, it will be up to you to decide how best to spend your money, how best to protect and preserve the backcountry environment and, if you choose, how best to help the people among whom you'll be traveling.

Alternative Travel

One way to travel responsibly is to sign up for an "alternative travel" tour. Since the concept of alternative travel is new, defining it is difficult. Alternative travel might mean participating in an organized peace tour through Communist Bloc countries. Or it might be an in-depth cultural tour far from Western-style hotels. For the backcountry enthusiast, alternative travel journeys may combine play with beneficial work. Earth Preservation Fund/Journeys, for instance, has involved its groups in such projects as reforestation in Peru, cleanups on Mount Everest and construction of solar cooking devices in Nepal and Ladakh.

Even if you choose a traditional tour rather than one that could be loosely defined as an alternative travel journey, you may wish to consider several factors when deciding what tour organization to sign up with. Does the organization you're considering show some awareness of environmental and cultural issues affecting the area of the world you'll be visiting? Does it offer you ample opportunity to interact with the locals? Will you be offered a realistic picture of the countries you visit, and will you be using the same modes of transportation and accommodation as the locals?

It's a good idea to ask the same questions of yourself even if you'll be traveling on your own. In fact, as an independent traveler, you can be especially in control of how you spend your money during your journey. Try to stay and to eat at small, family-owned hotels and restaurants, and to use the services provided by locals. That could mean hiring porters to carry your gear, having your laundry washed rather than doing it yourself, or spending 25 cents or so to get a shave in a barber shop.

The money you leave in the hands of a husband and wife who run a private hotel will do much more good for the locals than money left with a hotel owned by a multinational corporation. Buy local food rather than bringing freeze-dried food from home and, if possible, contract with porters on site rather than dealing with a Western-based tour agency.

It is just as important for you to pay close to market prices for local goods and services as it is for you to buy them in the first place. You actually do a disservice to the local community by paying far more than the going rate rather than bargaining for a better price. For example, by paying a porter twice as much as the going rate to carry your pack, you may feel as though you are being charitable. In fact, you are only reinforcing the view that the porter can make far more money working for Westerners than for the locals who must hire him to carry their goods to market. The porter cannot be blamed for refusing to carry his countryman's goods at the normal rate when just around the corner may be another rich Westerner willing to pay him twice as much for carrying a far lighter load. Likewise, paying more than market value for food you buy will only cause locals to refuse to sell their produce to other locals at a fair price, choosing to wait for Westerners instead.

Outdoor Ethics

Increasing numbers of North Americans are becoming concerned about responsible backcountry travel, wanting to preserve and protect North America's wilderness areas. It is even more crucial in the developing world, where natural resources like trees and water are being consumed at frightening rates—and where too many consumption-minded Westerners are reinforcing the idea that overuse in the interest of quick profit is quite acceptable.

Traveling responsibly in the backcountry of the developing world requires following the principles of minimum-impact camping, endeavoring to have as little impact as possible on your surroundings. Do all you can to preserve the backcountry environment you're experiencing so that those who follow may experience it too. In general, attempt to leave an area cleaner than you found it, and use as few natural resources as possible. The specific principles you may adopt when camping and backpacking include some obvious and some not-so-obvious ones.

First, don't litter. Of course, that means packing out whatever you pack in. Don't drop candy wrappers, cigarette butts or facial tissues on the trail, and don't leave them behind when you break camp. Don't be shy about picking up litter left behind by others either. Not so obviously, minimum-impact camping also requires disposing correctly of your toilet tissue and body wastes. Far from any water sources and away from trails, dig a hole at least six inches deep in which to bury your waste, and burn your toilet paper.

Second, select your campsites carefully. Try to find a site that has been used before, or has seating rocks already well spaced so you don't have to roll them into place, leaving ugly scars where they were. If you do move rocks, replace them when you leave. Select a site that has a spot for a tent which won't require a lot of rock or plant removal.

Third, use a cook stove except where downed fuelwood is plentiful. The dwindling supply of fuelwood in the backcountry of the developing world is a major problem. Don't worsen it for the sake of having a cheery evening fire. If you do have a campfire, build it in an already established fire ring. Or, if you build a fire ring, destroy it, bury the ashes from your fire, and scatter any leftover wood before leaving.

At all times in the backcountry, act in ways that will have the least impact on the environment. Don't cause erosion by walking off beaten paths. Avoid fuelwood-intensive hot showers at guest houses in areas where wood is scarce.

Begging

Sue and I sat with our backs against the pale blue wall of a small-town grocery store in Malawi. Beside us on the sidewalk sat a young man dressed in a clean shirt, a well-fitting sport coat and nice slacks. He played with a babbling baby in his lap. He and his baby were waiting with Sue and me for the morning bus. In studied, schoolboy English, the young man asked me where I was from. I answered, then leaned my head against the wall and relaxed. I fingered the few coins of tambala, the Malawian currency, in my pocket and wished the store offered something more than greasy balls of fried dough for breakfast. I was nearly dozing when I heard the young man beside me quietly reciting into the ear of his baby the same words that had been shouted at Sue and me by children everywhere we'd been in Malawi.

"Give me tambala," the young man was whispering over and over to the baby. "Give me tambala."

Begging is an integral part of many of the developing world's cultures. In some religions, giving to beggars is seen as an act of charity that helps the giver along the road to enlightenment or salvation. Add to that the fact that travelers through the years have proven themselves to be soft touches at the hands of beggars—especially children—and you'll know why you have to expect to be asked for money, candy or ballpoint pens.

Beggars can be exasperating. When approaching a village in Ladakh, backpackers are met with a chorus of shouts from children as soon as they come into view. The shouts follow them until they pass through town and are out of sight on the other side. Ladakh is popular with European hikers, so the children are multilingual in their requests. Candy is their main desire. They screech the words for it in every language they know: "Bonbon! Caramello! Candy!" over and over at the top of their lungs, with a "One pen!" thrown in now and then.

In contrast, trekkers have been walking the trails of Nepal far longer than they have those of Ladakh. All the trekking guidebooks to Nepal caution against giving in to the pleas of children, and the cautions have had their effect. Whereas in the past begging by children in Nepal was as pervasive as it is now in Ladakh, today it is much more subdued.

How should you handle the pleas of beggars? Don't give

in. It is best to leave giving to beggars to the locals. If you want to help in a particular instance, you may wish to leave pens or even money with the teacher at a local school. Your chances of doing some good are much enhanced by doing that rather than dropping a few coins in the hand of a cute little street urchin.

Ch. 8

It's the Water . . . And a Lot More

Digestive-tract illnesses are so much a part of travel in the developing world that you may be taking it for granted that you're going to get sick when you travel. And it's true that most people do indeed get sick during their journeys in the developing world. But it doesn't necessarily follow that you will be one of them.

Nothing makes a person feel farther from home than being sick while traveling. Nothing is more distressing, frustrating and time-consuming than a bad attack of diarrhea far from Mother's sympathy and chicken soup. But through care and diligence, you can avoid most of the serious illnesses that befall unwary and uninformed travelers. This chapter covers the developing world's most efficient sickness-causing substance—water—and what to do to keep it from making you ill.

First, some background.

In a series of armed conflicts in the 1960s and early 1970s, the Israeli Army repeatedly rolled over Egypt's armed forces. Time after time, the Israelis out-bombed, out-foxed and

out-fought the Egyptians. Then some astute scientific re-
searchers conducted studies that led them to believe that
Egypt's repeated losses were due at least partly to a parasitic
disease called schistosomiasis.

Schistosomes are little blood flukes that invade small
blood vessels near a person's intestines and bladder and
cause all sorts of trouble until they are flushed out by some
pretty strong drugs. Egypt, along with much of the rest of the
developing world, is infested with the parasites, which prey
mainly on humans living in rural areas, who come in contact
with open water regularly while irrigating, washing clothes,
drinking and bathing. Up to 90 percent of all Egyptians who
live in rural areas are afflicted with schistosomiasis. Most of
the Egyptian Army is made up of recruits from those same
rural areas. The result? A continually ill and lethargic army,
and a series of easy wins for Israel.

If that and other speculations are true, the '60s and '70s
in the Middle East marked only the latest victory for
schistosomiasis in the wars of man. In 1950 a widespread
attack of schistosomiasis is suspected of knocking the stuff-
ings out of the Chinese Communists before they could invade
the island of Taiwan in a planned assault. And during World
War II American troops were dragged down by schistosomes
during their fight to control the Philippines.

Aaron Klein, author of *The Parasites We Humans Harbor*,
writes: "During the last 25 years, most internal parasites of
man have been declining in status as major health problems.
The schistosomes, or blood flukes, however, have shown
every sign of going against this trend. In many parts of the
world there was an increase of schistosome infections in the
1970s."

The World Health Organization has named schistosomiasis one of the world's major health problems. To describe
where schistosomes are found is to describe the developing
world. Various versions of the parasite are found in many
parts of Africa, Asia and Latin America. The illness is known
as bilharziasis in much of Africa and as Katayama disease in
parts of the Far East.

Klein says Egyptians have been dealing with schistosomes for hundreds of years. Eggs from the fluke were found

in a 2,000-year-old Egyptian mummy. In recent years the schistosome problem has been compounded by the construction of the Aswan High Dam on the Nile River and the many irrigation projects emanating from it.

Schistosome eggs leave their human hosts through the hosts' feces and urine. The eggs hatch in fresh water and go through a larval stage in snails. When the larvae have developed, they leave the snails and bore directly through the skin of prospective human hosts who are either wading in or drinking from schistosome-infested water. The results are no fun. Fever, general malaise, abdominal pain, diarrhea, blocked blood vessels, enlarged organs and damaged intestinal walls are a few of schistosomiasis' dirty tricks. Untreated, the flukes live up to thirty years in the host's body.

It will be many years before the pollution of water by feces and urine in rural areas of the developing world ends. In the meantime it is impossible for rural people to avoid direct contact with their only source of survival—fresh water—even if it makes them sick at the same time.

You need not be included in this cycle, if you realize that the developing world's fresh water, no matter how crystalline looking, must always be considered suspect. If you picture tiny worms too small for you to see swimming around in that scoopful of cool water you're just about to pour down your parched throat—you won't be quite as thirsty as you were seconds earlier.

One other parasite is worthy of mention before we discuss prevention—giardia. The giardia parasite has gained notoriety in North America because of its relentless advance into the water sources of many of the United States' and Canada's wilderness areas and other uninhabited areas. From there, the persevering little bug has released cysts that have found their way into the drinking supplies of such notable mountain towns as Aspen, Colorado.

Giardiasis, commonly called traveler's diarrhea, is nowhere near as severe as schistosomiasis. But while it doesn't cause permanent internal damage, and doesn't last for thirty years, it still causes dangerously severe diarrhea, often of the explosive variety, so that those with the illness quickly learn to stay close to a handy place to relieve themselves. Although not as severe, giardiasis is much more common around the world than schistosomiasis. When you travel to the developing world—especially to its backcountry—you'll be almost sure to run into it somewhere along the way. If you fail to take the correct precautions, giardiasis is almost sure to hit you.

Giardia parasites, living in human and other mammalian hosts, form cysts that exit with the host's feces. As noted earlier, too often in the developing world feces find their way into waterways, and from there into drinking supplies. After the cysts are ingested, they hatch in the upper intestinal tract and begin multiplying. This results in nausea, gas and diarrhea, ranging from slight, if you're lucky, to severe, if you're not. The creation of thousands more cysts continues the cycle. Since many mammals carry giardia, no untreated water in the developing world—nor in North America's backcountry for that matter—can be considered safe from the parasite.

Maybe you still consider it a nuisance to have to be so diligent about purifying your water. If so, remember that giardia and schistosomes are simply the most prevalent of hundreds of harmful bacteria, protozoa, fungi and amebas which can be picked up from the waters of the developing world. *Dracunculus,* for example—known as the guinea worm—exists in all of the developing world except South America.

Guinea-worm larvae are ingested with drinking water via their intermediate hosts, microscopic shrimps. Once ingested, by humans, the larvae leave the shrimp and mature into worms up to 48 inches long which travel throughout the lower layers of the human host's skin. Klein writes that worms can sometimes be seen burrowing just under the skin, "somewhat like a rather mobile varicose vein." When they reach sexual maturity, the worms form ulcers in the skin through which they poke their heads. When the ulcer contacts water, the worm releases bursts of thousands of larvae, which are eaten by shrimp to continue the cycle.

When the worm pokes its head out in the open, its human host has a chance to attempt to remove it by wrapping it gently around a small stick, then continuing to wrap it further, if possible, until the entire worm is extracted. Surgical removal is also possible.

Prevention

First, it is fair to warn you that no matter how many precautions you take while visiting the developing world, you'll probably have loose stools during the beginning of your visit, and possibly throughout your stay. Most travelers find that whenever they go to a new country, their bodies go through an adjustment period to the new country's foods and unavoidable bacteria. During that time, they don't really feel ill, but their stools are loose and their timing is irregular. Generally after several days, however, their bodies make the necessary adjustments and their stools become firm and regular again.

It is also fair to warn you that despite your best efforts, you may come down with giardiasis or another serious intestinal problem during your stay. Such illnesses are so common in so much of the developing world that they can never be entirely avoided. A droplet of water on a piece of silverware, a hardy cyst that lives through the brief boiling of a pot of tea, a bit of water in the mouth while washing your hands and face—all can lead to illness.

Since Sue has worked as a medical technologist in the developing world, she has looked at more parasites and other tropical bugs under a microscope than most Westerners will ever see. She knows what the bugs will do to her, and she knows how to avoid them. Still, she managed to pick up giardia while we were backpacking in Malawi. In 12 hours she had more than 15 bowel movements and lost more than 10 pounds. We managed to reach a small town, where she received medical treatment from a doctor trained in the West, and we spent a week in the town's finest hotel reading and relaxing while Sue regained her strength.

That, unfortunately, is reality. But so is the fact that driving on the Interstate is dangerous. That doesn't keep you from driving, nor should the fear of getting ill dissuade you from taking what may well be the most exciting, enjoyable and adventurous vacation you'll ever experience.

Now, on to prevention. The rule is simple—avoid all water unless you know it to be pure. Don't be shy. If the silverware in a restaurant is damp, wipe it dry. And don't eat the fresh salad that has been served to you with dinner. Never eat uncooked foods unless you prepare them yourself using pure water, or unless you peel the food yourself, in the case of fruits. You may be derided by fellow travelers for leaving delectable looking and usually safe salads uneaten, but you'll also leave uneaten those salads that are not clean, and you'll remain healthy as a result.

The first step, then, toward staying healthy is to avoid all the impure water you can. The second is to purify all water you can't avoid. There are several methods of purifying, each of which has its pros and cons.

One way to purify water is to boil it. The method is fool-proof. It is also a time-consuming and fuel-intensive chore, since scientists have found that the toughest cysts can live up to 10 minutes in boiling water. With the need to boil water for 10 minutes, it is next to impossible to keep enough fuel on hand to do all the long-term boilings necessary to stay satiated.

Enter option two: chemicals. A tincture of iodine added to water will kill almost any organism lurking there. Several companies market iodine tablets and crystals for purifying water. Using them is a fairly easy method in that no stove is necessary, but the method is still time-consuming, since the water must sit 20–30 minutes after being treated before it is safe to drink.

Which brings us to option number three: filters. Filters have come into their own during the last few years, with the growth of the giardia problem in the wilderness areas of North America. The various filters available today use either gravity or a pump system to remove impurities from the water. The two most popular filters, both of which use a pump, are worth mentioning here. Both the *First-Need* water filter and the *Katadyn Pocket Filter* have been used extensively overseas.

The First-Need water filter weighs 12 ounces, half as much as the Katadyn. And at about $40 the First-Need costs less than one fourth as much. For that, you receive a "structured matrix" filter which traps impurities as small as giardia cysts. The First-Need's enclosed filter is in a cylinder about 4 inches long and 3 inches wide.

By contrast, the Katadyn weighs 23 ounces. It is about 2 inches wide and 8 inches tall. An article in *Backpacker* magazine called the Katadyn filter the "champagne" of water filters, and indeed it is. The Katadyn employs a ceramic filter whose 0.2 micron openings are more than 10 times smaller than the smallest giardia cyst. In addition to giardia, the Katadyn removes many other disease-causing bugs from drinking water, including typhoid germs, cholera germs and schistosomes. The Katadyn also removes all silt and algae. When it clogs, you simply remove its outer cover and wipe the raw-water side of the filter clean again. The literature included with the Katadyn says repeated cleanings eventually will wear down the filter to the point that it must be replaced. (When the C-shaped plastic piece included with the Katadyn will fit over the narrowest part of the filter, it's time to buy a new filter element.) After a year of almost daily use, however, including vigorous cleanings every few quarts, the filter Sue and I used on our trip showed little noticeable wear.

The First-Need's structured matrix filter is permanently enclosed. It can be unclogged by backwashing, but it cannot be cleaned entirely. As a result, the First-Need filter lasts through about 100 gallons of normal use. That's a lot of backpacking trips, but a person can go through 100 gallons quickly overseas. Replacement filter elements for the First-Need cost about $25.

The Katadyn costs close to $170. You'll probably never have to replace its ceramic filter element, but if you do, it'll run you about $100. You may want to consider buying the more expensive Katadyn filter if you expect to be in situations where the only water available is either laden with glacial silt or muddy from flooding. By cleaning your Katadyn over and over, you'll be able to live on clear, pure water. You have to let cloudy water settle before pumping it through a First-Need filter, and even then the filter will clog quickly.

If you choose to travel with a Katadyn, you'll most likely become a true believer in the letter from two Katadyn users which Katadyn proudly reprints as part of its sales pitch. "After two weeks of touring Africa," the letter reads, "the only students in our group who weren't sick were the two of us sharing a (Katadyn) water filter." Katadyn boasts that its filter is standard issue for UNICEF, the Indian Army, and Red Cross workers in disaster areas.

The best advantage of a water filter is that it is handy to use—it doesn't require waiting or boiling. For the Katadyn, however, the degree of ease of use is determined by how much you know about how to work the filter. Specific directions for its use are buried in the several pages of literature the company includes with the filter. And even after you've found them, the directions are unclear. As a result, many Katadyn users end up frustrated because they can't figure out how to make the filter work efficiently. If you're thinking of buying one, the following hints may prove invaluable.

It isn't easy to force water through the Katadyn's tiny pores. Rather than standing upright and holding the filter away from your body while pumping, as many dissatisfied customers try to do, brace the filter against the ground. Get down on one knee and hold the filter against your leg with one hand while keeping the other arm fairly straight and using it as a piston from the shoulder down to work the pump. That way, no great strength is necessary. Instead, the pumper's upper body weight forces the pump handle down.

Carry large-mouthed water bottles, which easily catch the Katadyn's stream of pure water. Put the impure water in a cook pot and pump from it. Leaving the filter's intake hose resting on the bottom of a lake or stream would allow it to suck up lots of debris, which would quickly clog the filter. In addition, if you pump directly from the source, you'll be on the uneven, muddy or rocky area at the water's edge, but if you dip a potful of water from the source, you can walk a few feet to a level area to pump. Also beneficial is cleaning the filter often and briskly. By cleaning the filter every few quarts—even more often when pumping dirty water—it's easy to keep the Katadyn pumping freely. Finally, remember that the ceramic filter will break if dropped on a hard surface, so be especially careful when you're cleaning it, and pad it well on plane rides and bus trips.

As giardia continues its advance in the lakes and streams

A backpacker on a section of the Inca Trail in Bolivia.

Travel in the developing world is remarkably affordable. Meals and lodging are inexpensive. Tribeswomen like the one here selling intricate bead bracelets in Kenya's Masai Mara National Park ask little for their handmade wares.

You'll be most readily accepted by the locals if you dress as conservatively as they do. A Ladakhi camp visitor shows here that pants are acceptable attire for women. In Nepal, local women wear only long skirts or dresses.

When you shop for food, you'll visit small shops or open markets like the outdoor market in Quito, Ecuador, pictured here.

The Himalayas, the Andes—including Peru's 19,122-foot Nevado Taulliraju pictured here—and numerous mountain ranges in Africa, Asia and South America offer limitless backpacking and camping possibilities. The deserts and jungles of the developing world also provide untold opportunities for the intrepid traveler.

Despite the neatness of this Peruvian farm, poverty still exists here and in most rural areas of the developing world. Chronic diarrhea, tuberculosis and malnutrition haunt rural inhabitants throughout Africa, Asia and South America.

A woman washes clothes in a shantytown outside Quito, Ecuador. Poverty afflicts some 60 percent of the people of the developing world.

During your travels, avoid any animal whose bite can break your skin. Although the dog shown here playing with a group of children in Ecuador probably doesn't have rabies, if it happened to nip you, you'd have to assume that it could have the disease.

Sampling an area's native dishes like these fried grasshoppers in Bangkok, Thailand, will be one of the most fascinating—and adventurous—aspects of your journey.

A Bolivian woman in her bowler hat pauses on a trail high in the Andes.

English is the world's most international language, as this sign in Nepal's back-country attests.

of North America, more water filters are being designed and offered for sale. Check into the latest filters on the market before buying one.

When you're overseas, you'll probably depend on a combination of boiling, adding chemicals and filtering to purify your water. If you'll be doing your own cooking, you won't need to worry about filtering the water you use to boil potatoes or simmer soup for more than 10 minutes. You'll need to carry iodine with you at all times as a back-up to your filter should it be stolen or broken. Your mainstay, however, most likely will be your water filter, which you'll use almost daily.

The water in most of the developing world's cities, although generally clear, is not safe to drink. Don't let the fact that it is coming out of a modern faucet fool you, nor that others are quaffing cupful after cupful. Always purify your drinking water, even the little you use for brushing your teeth. Kathmandu, for example, is known for the giardia that infest its water every monsoon season. Since the city is well known for its giardia woes, restaurant owners in Kathmandu advertise that all the water they use has been boiled for at least 30 minutes. But unless you can verify their claims, you'll be better off putting up with the minor inconvenience of eating only cooked foods and of pumping your own pure water to drink with your meal rather than take the chance of being ill for several weeks.

Boiled drinks like tea and coffee are generally safe to drink, as are commercially bottled drinks like sodas and juices—but don't have any with ice! Bottled water is also available in cities. Be sure any bottles you buy are sealed. Entrepreneurs interested in quick profits rather than the health of their clients have been known to fill used water bottles with tap water, recap them with used lids and sell them as new. With hot drinks, there is always the chance that the water wasn't boiled for 10 minutes, and that a giardia cyst managed to survive. But you've got to draw the line somewhere. However, do note, where possible, how the dishes are washed. If they are being washed in cold water, pull out your own plastic mug and plate and ask that the restaurateur serve you in them, or wipe the cup and plate dry.

You may find such behavior embarrassing at first, but as

time goes on you'll realize that your language, clothing and manners are all so unusual to those who are serving you that asking to use your own cup, drinking from your own bottle of water or passing up uncooked foods is not considered rude. Rather, your actions will simply be accepted as another facet of your uniqueness.

In addition to being sure to ingest only pure water as much as possible by purifying your water and by avoiding uncooked foods and wet dishware, there are other ways to avoid getting ill from the developing world's water.

First, some of the hardier parasites, the most common of which are schistosome larvae, will actually drill through your skin if given the chance. You can help deny them that chance by always wearing thongs or plastic sandals in the shower. You don't need to worry about the water coming out of the shower head. Rather, the danger is the water already on the floor of the shower stall. The warm, moist climate of a shower stall provides a good environment for parasite larvae to stay alive while waiting for a host to come along. Don't come along barefoot and you'll be fine.

Also, avoid swimming in schistosome-infested water, or water suspected of being infested. Try to live by the adage, "When in doubt, stay out." It's easy to say that to yourself now, but when you come upon a beautiful pond fringed by palm trees after hiking in 100-degree heat for hours, it's tough advice to follow. Just think of all those little parasites playing havoc with your insides—those thoughts will do wonders for your will power. If you must wade or swim across a watercourse you suspect is infested, use a cloth as soon as you emerge to wipe down whatever parts of your body are wet. A quick, thorough wipedown should catch the larvae before they have a chance to get into your skin. The larvae won't survive more than a few minutes out of water, so your cloth won't be infected by them the next time you use it.

Some studies have found that taking an antibiotic or Pepto-Bismol as a preventive may be effective in fighting off the developing world's many unavoidable minor bacterial strains. However, results of the studies have been inconclusive, and there are problems with taking both antibiotics and Pepto-Bismol. The problem with taking an antibiotic as a preventive is that each time you do so you reduce the ability of any particular antibiotic to fight a real bacterial illness in your system should you come down with one. A study on Pepto-Bismol found that, for most people, the drug is beneficial as a preventive only when taken in large doses several times a day.

The next chapter, on health, is more specific about sickness prevention and cure through drugs. By far your best bet, however, is to do all in your power to stay healthy in the first place. Being in good physical condition when you go to the developing world and following the preventive guidelines laid out in this chapter and the next are the best ways to avoid spending several days trundling back and forth between your bed and the nearest toilet, or being otherwise incapacitated.

Ch. 9

Health

If you get sick overseas, you will get better. However, you want to avoid getting sick in the first place. This even includes doing the right things to avoid contracting any of the diseases for which you may already have been vaccinated before you started your journey. For example, a gamma globulin shot only boosts your immune system to help in its attempt to fight off hepatitis. To avoid hepatitis altogether, you must diligently avoid unclean food, water and eating utensils.

Just as it is important to eat only clean foods and to drink only clean water, so it is imperative that you stay physically clean. Hands are great collectors and dispensers of germs. Cleaning and drying them before every meal—even without soap—will help to keep them from dispensing germs into your mouth. Keep your feet clean and dry to prevent athlete's-foot fungus, especially when you're on the trail. Never go barefoot unless you want to run the risk of contracting hookworm. Body lice are prevalent in much of the developing world, but keeping your clothing, gear and body as clean as possible will help fend them off. For women, especially those prone to vaginal infections, personal hygiene is mandatory. Wearing a skirt so you can wash yourself without disrobing is convenient in places where only semi-privacy is possible.

Before You Leave

Before you leave on your journey, you should:

• *Get all the vaccinations necessary for the area you'll be visiting. See Ch. 4 for details.*

• *Check your medical insurance policy to be sure you're covered while you're overseas. If you don't have medical insurance for overseas, be sure to get it before you go. The least expensive way is to sign up for a policy with a high deductible— up to $2,000 is possible.*

• *If you'll be traveling long, have your teeth checked. Qualified dentists are rare and expensive in the developing world.*

• *Leave your contact lenses at home. You could travel with contact lenses in the developing world, but they are difficult to keep clean,especially in the backcountry. Carry a copy of your lens prescription in case you lose your glasses or your contacts.*

• *Meet with your doctor or with a doctor in a large-city hospital's clinic for international travelers. Discuss any special medicines or precautions the doctor may recommend, and get prescriptions for the special medicines you decide to carry in your medical kit and for any regular medicines you may need to stock up on. When buying medicines, be sure to shop around. Some of the items you'll be buying may be quite expensive, and prices of prescription medicines vary greatly in the U.S. Buy the generic forms of various medicines you want if available.*

• *Contact the International Association for Medical Assistance to Travelers, at 417 Center Street, Lewiston, NY 14092. IAMAT provides a list of English-speaking doctors who are on call 24 hours a day in many developing countries. These doctors have a set fee schedule. All the IAMAT doctors are located in large cities, however, so they'll be able to help you only if you conveniently get sick while in one. IAMAT also publishes information on malaria risk areas.*

After you return, have your stool examined, even if you didn't have diarrhea on your trip. Many parasites and bacteria take a while to make their presence known. If discovered early, they're easily treated, but once they've taken hold, treatment is more difficult. Be sure the person

examining your stool knows why you're having it checked, so
he or she will know to look for any unusual organisms.

Feet—Athlete's Foot and Blisters

If you are at all prone to athlete's foot, bring a small
amount of athlete's-foot treatment with you. An ointment
called NP-27 is especially powerful—a tiny bit of the foul-
smelling stuff goes a long way. Carry only a small plastic vial's
worth to save both weight and space.

Moleskin has been the blister pad of choice for years, but
you might try some other product. For example, Spenco
markets a blister pad that incorporates a moist second skin
held in place by a sticky pad. Use the pad before blisters
start. If you feel a hot spot on your heel or elsewhere on your
foot, stop and treat it right away, despite the guilt you may
feel at holding up the rest of your group. If you don't, you
may be holding them up a lot more when your blisters get bad
later.

Don't leave a blister pad on for too long. Your skin will rot
beneath it. If you take it off 48 hours or so later, the pad may
take a layer of skin with it and you'll be far worse than when
you started. Use the pads only when you'll be walking. Allow
your blisters or hot spots to heal at all other times by carefully removing your pads. You may go through quite a few
pads, so be sure to bring enough to last out your trip.

Skin—Sunburn and Chapped Skin

Unless you want a tan, carry the strongest sunscreen you
can find. The cream variety stretches the furthest. Sunscreen
lip balm is nice to have along too. Be especially attentive
when walking on snow, when the sun's rays reflecting from
below may actually burn your face, even when shaded by a
visor. Wear sunglasses in such conditions as well, to avoid
headaches later in the day.

In addition to sunburn, chapped skin may be a problem,
especially in dry climates or as a companion problem to
another illness. For example, you may end up with a chapped

nose while you're suffering from a cold, or—more likely and more distressing—an even more tender part of your anatomy may end up raw after a bout with diarrhea or even a series of intestinal gas releases (common on high-altitude treks). The best way to treat these is with generous applications of petroleum jelly. You'll use the jelly for lots of other reasons as well, from lubricating a cook-stove to helping free a stuck zipper. Bring the jelly in a leakproof container. Skin lotion is also nice to have along, but it's heavy and doesn't go far.

If you're prone to any other skin-related problems, like rashes, hemorrhoids, cold sores, canker sores or vaginal infections, bring along treatment ointments for those as well.

Cold—Hypothermia and Frostbite

Hypothermia occurs when the body's core temperature drops. It can happen at temperatures well above freezing when wind and wetness combine with insufficient clothing to overcome the body's ability to heat itself. Initially, a hypothermia victim is pale, shivering, apathetic, clumsy and confused. As hypothermia progresses, the victim's speech becomes slurred and walking becomes difficult. Eventually the shivering will stop and the victim will suffer memory lapses and hallucinations. If swift action is not taken, the victim will lapse into unconsciousness, and death will follow.

Once hypothermia has set in, the only way for a victim to recover is to be exposed directly to an external source of heat. In minor cases a fire may be sufficient. But in severe cases the victim must be put in the shelter of a building, tent or snow cave, the victim's wet clothing must be removed, and a naked companion must join the victim in a sleeping bag for warmth.

Frostbite is the freezing of external parts of the body, rather than an overall loss of body heat. Generally, only extremely cold temperatures cause frostbite, but ill-prepared backpackers and hikers in high-altitudes have suffered from it. To prevent frostbite at a high pass or on a cold day, be sure you're adequately clothed and are wearing correct footwear. Eat well and drink plenty of liquids, since lack of energy and dehydration both contribute to the onset of frostbite. Frostbite attacks the body's extremities. For the inexperienced, the toes are in the greatest danger. Never let your toes go numb while walking. If they are approaching numbness, stop to warm them against the body of a member of your party. In actual frostbite, the affected area will be white or blue. Immediate action is required. Use warm water to warm the affected area slowly. After that, the victim must be evacuated to receive further medical treatment.

Heat—Heat Exhaustion, Dehydration and Sunstroke

Travelers to hot areas of the developing world are susceptible to several heat-related maladies, including heat exhaustion, dehydration and sunstroke. The least worrisome of these is heat exhaustion, which results when the victim simply tries to do too much too fast in a climate that is far hotter than that to which he or she is accustomed. Prevention is obvious—don't try to do and see everything at once. Plan to come back later to see what you missed the first time around. Just as important, drink lots of liquids. It is very easy to become dehydrated in the developing world. The lack of air conditioning in most city buildings causes your body's air-conditioning system—perspiration—to move into high gear. In the backcountry you'll lose even more body fluids through perspiration. You'll be tempted to put off drinking even your normal amount of liquids, much less the doubled or tripled level of intake your body may require, because of the hassle of obtaining purified liquids, but giving in to such temptation can lead to the debilitating headaches and stomach cramps of acute dehydration.

Treatment of heat exhaustion calls for lying down out of the sun and drinking lots of fluids. The same is true for treating dehydration. You may also wish to increase your salt intake during the parts of your trip when you perspire a great deal.

Whereas dehydration most often is a problem in low-humidity areas where the dry outdoor environment steals your body's fluids, sunstroke often occurs in areas of high humidity, when your body's cooling system fails because your perspiration does not evaporate in the humid air. The sunstroke victim stops perspiring and becomes delirious. The victim's temperature climbs, and eventually he or she will fall into a coma. To offset the effects of sunstroke, the victim must be taken to a shaded spot and cool, wet towels or cloths applied to the body.

The best way to prevent sunstroke is to take it easy. Don't be tempted to overdo it in muggy climates.

Height—Altitude Sickness

If you'll be traveling at high altitudes during your journey, there is no way to overstress the importance of the following information. Altitude sickness is a killer. Travelers die each year because they didn't take seriously the effects of high altitude. The list of fatalities invariably includes experienced mountaineers and doctors, as well as first-time visitors to high altitudes who succumb due to lack of knowledge and a false sense of their own infallibility. Altitude sickness can affect anyone, from marathon runners and weight lifters to the obese and the normally sedentary. In a way, being in good shape can actually be a drawback. If you've worked out and are physically ready for your mountain trekking adventure, you may be tempted to ascend faster than you should. While others may be able to handle only 1,000 feet of elevation gain per day, you may feel fine while climbing 3,000 feet or so per day—until the effects of altitude sickness come crashing down.

Acute altitude sickness can set in at altitudes as low as 8,000 feet, and it can result in death within hours. The best treatment by far for it is rapid descent—which may be difficult or, in some cases, impossible. Instead, prevention is the key to avoiding acute altitude sickness altogether.

The national park rangers of Mt. Kenya say that their mountain has the highest incidence of acute altitude sickness of any single place on earth—despite the fact that the mountain's top, at just over 17,000 feet, is lower than many passes hikers traverse in the Himalayas beneath 20,000–29,000-foot peaks. This is because the difference in elevation between the

Kenyan plain and the top of the peak—more than 10,000 feet—can be covered in as little as a day and a half by any healthy hiker.

The human body must be allowed to acclimate to higher altitudes gradually. You must give your body time to adjust to the lack of oxygen at your present altitude before you climb higher, even if you feel perfectly fine and are eager to get moving. Another prevention aid is to drink plenty of liquids. Try to drink at least a gallon a day—enough to keep your urine almost clear. Brightly colored urine means you're not drinking enough.

When acclimating, the general rule is to climb an average of no more than 1,000–1,500 feet per day at altitudes above 10,000 feet. Yet most healthy hikers can easily gain 3,000 feet per day. If you wish to do so, you'll need to take a break at your present altitude for a day or two before continuing. If you feel good, you may climb higher during your rest day before returning to your lower camp to sleep.

In situations like climbing Mt. Kenya, which could take as long as a week to climb by following the 1,000-foot-per-day rule, you may be able to climb and return to lower elevations quickly before altitude-sickness symptoms have a chance to set in. Himalayan climbers in recent years have popularized this approach to climbing extremely high peaks. But many have paid the price of such risky undertakings. Whenever you climb at a rate of more than 1,000–1,500 feet per day at high elevations, you run a risk of contracting acute altitude sickness. You should do this only if you are a member of a party large enough to help you or anyone else who becomes ill, and if you are entirely willing to turn around and descend at any sign of acute altitude sickness.

Diagnosing acute altitude sickness is especially tricky, because virtually everyone who travels to high altitudes—12,000–14,000 feet and above—will experience minor symptoms of altitude sickness. It is crucial for you to know when those minor symptoms become acute.

Minor symptoms of altitude sickness include an upset stomach, loss of appetite, lightheadedness, dizziness, mild shortness of breath while walking, and disturbed sleep. These minor symptoms are warning signals. You may experience some of them as you move upward. They will generally abate during your one or two rest days before you climb higher. If they do not, stay a day or two longer at your present altitude until they abate, then climb higher. If even that extra wait doesn't help, you should descend to whatever altitude is necessary to relieve your symptoms. After a day or two there, you may wish to try climbing slowly once again, since altitude sickness may affect your body differently each time you ascend to high altitudes. The fact that you've not had trouble at high altitudes in the past does not mean you can ascend quickly the next time. Caution is the only way to avoid acute altitude sickness.

The symptoms of acute altitude sickness are simply more severe manifestations of the minor ones. That's why it is especially important to watch for them when you are already suffering from minor symptoms. As acute altitude sickness sets in, the victim will become testy and confused, so it is up to all members of a party to keep an eye on one another.

The more severe symptoms of acute altitude sickness include shortness of breath even after resting; wet, bubbly breathing; rapid heart rate; severe coughing, possibly including the spitting up of blood; severe headache; vomiting; apathy and confusion; loss of coordination; and, finally, coma. After the onset of any of these symptoms, death may soon follow. The best treatment is for the victim to descend as far as possible as quickly as possible—preferably on a stretcher or on the back of a porter. Rapid recovery often follows a rapid descent of several thousand feet. Recovery may be so complete, in fact, that the victim may wish to try ascending again—at a very slow rate.

Bites—Malaria, Rabies and Bedbugs

Like altitude sickness, malaria is a malady that many travelers do not take seriously. Since mosquitos, including females of the anopheles species that transmit malaria, are more prevalent in the backcountry than in the cities, where spraying programs often cut back on the number of mosquitos, backcountry travelers must be especially aware of the risk of malaria.

Trying to get information on how and when to guard against malaria is difficult. Countries where the parasite exists (that includes most of the developing world) have no desire to scare away tourists by headlining their malaria problems in their tourist-information brochures. Gathering information on the disease in the U.S., where it is rarely seen and little known, is not much easier.

Yet you must learn whether malaria is a problem in any of the areas you plan to visit. Your specific guidebooks should have that information, as should any international-traveler clinic or big-city vaccination center. In addition, the International Association for Medical Aid to Travelers provides information on malaria, including where the parasite is prevalent and how to avoid it. (IAMAT's address is provided in the "Before You Leave" section earlier in this chapter.) The boundaries between where malaria is prevalent and where it is not are always shifting. Base your decision on the most recent information you can find.

Before you can fully consider what precautions to take against malaria, you must learn whether chloroquine-resistant malaria is present in the areas you plan to visit. Until recently, the drug chloroquine taken as a preventive had been enormously successful in combating the malaria parasite after people were bitten. But chloroquine's success was also its downfall. The drug was so successful that everyone started taking it. Relief agencies handed it out in many places to locals. After a while, the malaria parasites began mutating, until now a chloroquine-resistant strain is spreading through the developing world. The medical community is scrambling to develop safe drugs to combat the new strain.

In the meantime, you must try to figure out what to do. Again, base your decision on the latest information you can find. Probably your best bet is to ask the advice of a doctor at one of the international travel clinics set up by hospitals in cities across the U.S.

Whatever antimalarial drugs you end up packing, you'll most likely be told to start taking them two weeks before you enter a malaria-risk area and up to six weeks after you leave.

The best thing of all, of course, is to avoid being bitten by the anopheles mosquito. Luckily, the anopheles flies only at night. From dusk until dawn, wear long pants and a long-sleeved shirt, and keep any exposed skin well covered with insect repellent. Any of the powerful repellents now on the market is adequate. Use liquid, not spray. A can of spray is heavy and bulky and lasts about a week, whereas a two-ounce bottle of liquid will last next to forever. Just a few drops spread on your skin will keep the bugs at bay. The repellent eats up nylon, Gore-Tex and the like, so let it dry on your skin before donning your rain parka.

When camping, be sure your tent is mosquito-free as you settle down for the night, and keep your screen door zipped tight. When staying in a hotel or a guest house in a malaria-risk area, get a room that either is screen-sealed or has mosquito netting over the beds. Tape or small bandages is good for closing up the holes you'll invariably find in the screens or the netting. If no mosquito-free rooms are available, your options include burning one of the mosquito coils available in much of the developing world, covering all exposed areas of your skin with repellent before you go to sleep, and rigging up your tent like a mosquito net inside the room. Unless you'll be spending a lot of time in cities, it won't be worth your while to carry your own mosquito net.

While malaria is prevalent in most of Latin America, Africa and Asia, by far the highest percentage of Western travelers contract the disease in East Africa, where the parasite is rife. Some travelers find it adventurous to actually risk malaria by being lax about taking their antimalaria pills and by not avoiding mosquito bites. Don't follow their foolish lead. Do all you can to avoid being bitten by a mosquito, and take your pills religiously. One strain of malaria attacks the brain, and can kill within hours. Most malaria strains are not so virulent, but once you've had the disease, in most cases it will recur throughout your life. The onset of malaria is like a severe bout with the flu. If you suspect you have malaria, you should seek medical assistance immediately. Malaria is generally treated with large amounts of the same drugs you took to prevent it in the first place.

While not nearly as prevalent as malaria, rabies still exists in much of the developing world. Don't feed friendly squirrels or other animals, avoid ratty-looking hotels, and don't pet any dogs. In areas with many dogs, you may wish to carry a stick or a handful of rocks to fend off any particularly vicious dogs. If you are bitten by an animal, the wound must penetrate the skin for the animal's saliva to pass rabies on to you. If that happens, wash out the wound immediately. Next, evaluate the circumstances surrounding the bite. Most animal bites are by dogs. Did you surprise a dog when you came through a gate or around a corner? If so, and if the dog seemed to be healthy after the attack, you'll most likely be all right. If you wish to make sure, check on the health of the dog a week to 10 days later—if it is alive, you're going to live. In the case of a small animal bite or an unexplainable dog bite, your actions should be a little more dramatic. Try to capture the animal. If it remains healthy for a week, you're home free. If you're unable to capture the offending animal and you're worried about the circumstances surrounding the bite, or if the offending animal becomes ill or dies, to be absolutely sure of not contracting rabies you have no choice but to get to a large city quickly and take the course of rabies vaccinations.

Bedbugs put a damper on a lot more trips to the developing world than malaria and rabies combined. You may run across the little devils in the ritziest as well as the least expensive hotels and guest houses. If you run across them in a nice hotel, inform the management and change rooms. The hotel staff most likely will insist that all that is necessary is a change of sheets, but bedbugs are aware of this trick. They're likely to hide in cracks in the bedframe or on the floor until the lights go out. Instead, change rooms. If the second room is no better than the first, change hotels. On the trail or in small towns, where choice of hotels and guest houses is limited and you fear an after-dark bedbug invasion, use your unerected tent as a protective layer between the bed and you, and sleep in your sleeping bag. In a worst-case scenario, you may wish to actually sleep inside your tent, with its netted door zipped tight. In almost any guest house on the trail, bedding is not provided. Instead, you use your own bedding on a well-used foam pad in the house's dormitory-style sleeping room. In the interest of cleanliness and disease prevention as well as bedbug avoidance, use your tent as a bed cover and sleep atop it in all such situations.

Accidents—Cuts, Scrapes, Twists, Strains

You'll invariably suffer a few minor cuts and scrapes in the backcountry. For each one follow normal first-aid procedure—wash the wound, then treat and bandage it, no matter how small the wound. Infection will get started a lot easier in an unclean, exposed wound in the developing world than in a similar wound that might or might not be worthy of a bandaid at home. Wash any wounds with soap and water, carry a small amount of topical antibiotic cream to treat wounds, and carry bandaids plus some adhesive tape and gauze for larger wounds.

Keep in mind that you'll have a lot more trouble overcoming the difficulties posed by a pulled muscle or sprained ankle overseas than you would a mile from home during your daily run. Hence you should think before you act during your journey. Are you faced with walking down a steep, muddy slope? Consider your options: Linking arms with a partner may make you both more stable. Perhaps the slope is steep enough that it is worth letting your pack down by rope, freeing you to clamber down safely without it on your back. Or, if you choose to work your way down the slope while wearing your pack, pick your footholds before you move forward, and plan how and where you'll fall if you slip. In tricky situations, always adjust your weight so that, if you fall, you'll fall into the slope, preferably on your backside.

If you do pull a muscle or twist an ankle, the best treatment is rest. Don't let your pride cause you to injure yourself further. Share your load with others. Fashion yourself a crutch and limp along as you heal.

Respiratory—Runny Noses, Colds and Flu

We've grown accustomed to the Asian, the Russian or some other flu invading our borders and slapping thousands of us with influenza each winter. That happens because each year's particular flu virus is one our bodies are unfamiliar with, so that we have no antibodies built up against it. That being true, it is clear why colds and the flu plague many travelers to the developing world, where countless viruses wait to play havoc with their unsuspecting bodies. To avoid being one of the many, keep your body in shape during your journey, to help it fight off all that attacks it. Get plenty of sleep, eat well and drink lots of liquids. Carry antihistamine to help fight the sniffles or blocked sinuses. Aspirin will help with the aches and pains of a cold or the flu. It will also help you deal with the occasional headache you may suffer from a day in the bright sun.

Intestinal—Diarrhea, Constipation

Within the intestinal tract, everyone harbors naturally occurring bacteria. Each of our bodies is accustomed to those bacterial strains that are normal for our area. When we go abroad, our intestinal tracts suddenly are exposed to unaccustomed bacterial strains. Some of these are quite virulent. They are what cause the loose stools most travelers experience in a new country. They are also responsible for most of the cases of diarrhea—numerous loose stools each day—that befall travelers in the developing world. Parasites, most often giardia, are responsible for many of the remaining cases of diarrhea along with a few more serious illnesses.

As mentioned at the end of the last chapter, taking either antibiotics or Pepto-Bismol in an attempt to fend off intestinal illnesses before they strike probably is not worthwhile. By being careful about what you eat and drink, you'll most likely avoid the more serious intestinal illnesses. If you do have loose stools, be sure to drink lots of liquids to avoid becoming dehydrated. Taking Pepto-Bismol tablets will help your stools to become firm again. Eventually your body will settle its disagreements with the new country's strange bacteria on its own.

What if you develop a severe case of diarrhea, with numerous bowel movements every day, all of which are liquid in consistency? First, *don't* take any drugs that stop the digestive tract's operation. That would stop your diarrhea, but it might also harm you. A few of the more virulent intestinal illnesses give off dangerous levels of toxins, which are safely flushed out of your system when you have diarrhea. Halting your bowel movements would trap those toxins in your body.

Among the traveling crowd, a drug called Lomotil is widely used against diarrhea, but unfortunately it shuts down your intestinal system, trapping whatever is making you sick. Diarrhea is one of the body's ways of fighting off a serious bug. Don't halt its attempts to do so.

The most important thing to do if you're suffering from diarrhea is to stay well-hydrated. A serious bout of diarrhea can reduce your body fluids to dangerously low levels in only a few hours. In addition to losing fluids rapidly when you have diarrhea, you lose nutrients that would normally be re-absorbed by the body during the digestive process. Glucose (found in sugar) and sodium (found in salt) are two that your body needs to survive. To battle diarrhea, drink as much liquid as you can and increase your intake of sugar and salt.

Several antibiotic medications will work for intestinal ill-nesses. Tetracycline and erythromycin both work against many diarrhea-causing bacteria. They are also widely used in the U.S. to fight acne-causing bacteria, so they are affordable and easy to find. Doxycycline is another antibiotic often pre-scribed by doctors to fight bacterial diarrhea. It is expensive, but many feel it works against more forms of bacterial diarrhea than tetracycline or erythromycin. Discuss what may work best for you with your regular physician or with a doctor working at a large hospital's international-traveler clinic. The latter most likely will be more up-to-date on the latest antidiarrheal antibiotics.

No one can say definitely which antibiotics work best. It all depends on you and the particular strain of bacterial diarrhea you pick up. When taking antibiotics, it is important to take them for five to seven days even if your diarrhea clears up earlier, so the drugs can clean up all the diarrhea-causing bacteria in your body.

If your diarrhea persists for more than a week, or is accompanied by burps or intestinal gas that smells like rotten eggs, you may well have giardiasis. The best way to find out is to have a sample of your stool examined by a medical laboratory. (However, giardia cysts are released by the body in bursts, so not every bowel movement may contain them.) If you suspect giardia, try to seek medical attention. However, since giardia is fairly common but medical aid may be far away, you may wish to carry an antiparasitic drug prescribed by a doctor to treat suspected giardia in the backcountry. Antiparasitic drugs are strong medication, and should be taken only if giardia is strongly suspected and medical assistance is not available.

Dysentery is diarrhea that includes blood or mucus in the stool. It often involves vomiting and fever as well. If you are stricken with dysentery, it is unlikely you'll be able to continue your travels (as you may well be able to with diarrhea). Instead, seek medical assistance as quickly as possible.

While everyone else is fighting diarrhea, you could end up constipated. The lack of clean toilet facilities and the difficulty of keeping up your liquid intake can bring that about. If you do find yourself constipated, deluge yourself with liquids and natural laxatives like fruit or tea. And be thankful you don't have diarrhea.

Remember, all drugs, including antibiotics, have potential side effects. Know them before deciding which antibiotics are for you. Tetracycline, for example, is known to make some people's skin sensitive to sunburn, and some antibiotics should not be taken if you are pregnant. As for dosages, when you get your prescriptions, your doctor will note correct dosages.

If You Need Medical Assistance

Finding a doctor in a large city of a developing country is relatively easy. You may contact an IAMAT-member doctor if one practices in that city. (See the "Before You Leave" section earlier in this chapter.) You may also contact the American or Canadian embassy or consulate if the city has one. Duty officers there, on duty 24 hours a day, have lists of English-speaking doctors who practice in the area. If there are no IAMAT-member doctors or North American embassies or consulates in the city, ask the front desk of one of the large Western-style hotels in the city for the names of doctors they suggest for their English-speaking guests. You may also ask for references from any international aid organizations in the city.

Finding medical assistance in the backcountry is more

problematic. Many group tours give discounts to doctor-participants who act as medics for tour members. If you're on your own, however, and you're in an area where few other travelers venture, it will be up to the members of your party to get you to a place where medical aid is available. If you're in a more popular area of the backcountry, you may contact the field offices of any international aid organizations in the area or ask any tour group if there is a doctor in their group.

Suggested Medical Kit List

You may wish to carry some or all of the following things in your medical kit. The suggestions are based on the explanations provided earlier in this chapter. Remember, the information contained in this chapter and in the following list is general in scope. To determine exactly which items will be best for your medical kit, how much of each you should carry, and correct dosages, you must seek the advice of a physician experienced in international travel.

Athlete's foot ointment
Blister pads
Cream sunscreen
Sunscreen lip balm
Petroleum jelly
Skin lotion
Medications for personal skin-related problems
Insect repellent
Antimalarial medication
Topical antibiotic ointment
Bandaids
Adhesive tape and gauze
Antihistamine
Aspirin
Pepto-Bismol tablets
Antibiotics
Antiparasitic drug

Ch. 10

Food

Shopping for food with the locals and sampling an area's native entrees, side dishes, drinks and desserts—which may range from succulent boiled crabmeat to fried grasshopper—will be one of the most fascinating and enjoyable aspects of your journey.

When preparing your own food, you'll need to take health precautions. Peel all uncooked foods or wash them in pure water and dry them before eating. The washing method isn't foolproof, but it's a lot better than just biting into an apple or a carrot having only wiped it on your shirt. When boiling foods, boil them for at least 10 minutes. The same, of course, is true when boiling water for tea or coffee, unless you've purified it beforehand.

If you'll be preparing your own food in the backcountry, you'll have no problem buying and eating the same foods as those available to locals. It'll take some perseverance on your part to learn the local currency, the market value of various foods and where to find what you want in stores and markets, but the experience of doing so will more than make up for the frustrations. On short trips, you could bring some or all of your backpacking food with you from home, but it is far more interesting to eat the local diet. You need not be worried about getting enough protein from the diet that awaits you if you'll be cooking your own food overseas. While meat and meat products are generally scarce, expensive, and fly-ridden or spoiled, people living in the developing world know what to eat to achieve a balanced diet. Some protein-rich mixture of beans and rice is evident in much of the developing world. In Latin America, refried beans and fried rice are standard fare. In Asia, boiled lentils and rice are common. Only in sub-Saharan Africa, where bananas or boiled corn flour is often the basic food, can protein deficiency become a problem. And even there, lack of protein will become a concern only over time.

During your journey, how you buy your food will be determined in large part by where you are. If you're buying food in a large city, your choices will range from the rare large supermarket to the more common small food stores, which sell basics like rice, beans, potatoes, sugar and various flours by weight from burlap sacks sitting on the floor. Shelves on the walls are stocked with things like canned margarine, shortening, hard candy, chocolate, peanut butter, jam, powdered milk, tea, oatmeal and instant coffee. In addition, such stores carry a smattering of things like socks, laundry detergent, flashlights, batteries, candles, writing pens and notebook paper. Tiny bakeries hide behind worn doors in every community. You'll be able to locate them by the smell of their freshly made goods, and buy stacks of hot tortillas or loaves of warm bread wrapped in newspaper.

In smaller towns less is available. However, a wide enough variety of food will probably be available in even the smallest towns to satisfy you—provided the town is connected by road to larger cities. Once you're on the trail, in most cases, you'll be able to buy only those foods grown locally. The exception is along popular trekking routes, where stores and guest houses are often stocked with essentials like toilet paper and treats like candy and chocolate. Since those items must be delivered by porter or animal, their prices are commensurately higher than goods delivered by truck in road-connected cities and towns.

If you are going to any areas where food availability may be questionable, be sure to ask ahead. If there is any doubt, carry enough food into the backcountry to last the length of time you plan to stay.

If you munch on sweets whenever you're on the trail, don't give in to the pleas of children for treats. The same goes for cigarettes to adults. The introduction of sugar-laden Western candy into the diets of the developing world has led to extensive tooth decay. Those who eat the candy do not know how to protect themselves against decay, and they cannot have their damaged teeth repaired. Likewise, the introduction of tobacco has drastically lowered the life expectancy rates of many peoples of developing nations.

If you'll be cooking for yourself, you must consider fuel as well as food. Before you head into the backcountry, learn what foods will be available along the trail and in what quantities. Use that information to decide how much fuel you'll need to carry. If you take oatmeal for breakfast, your breakfast cooking time will be short; if you'll be boiling rice to make rice pudding for breakfast, your cooking time will be three to four times longer.

Fuel is one of the heaviest things you carry on backpacking trips. To conserve fuel, soak hard foods overnight before cooking. This may mean having beans and rice in the morning and oatmeal at night, but on a long trip the fuel you save will be worth such unusual eating habits.

Eating Out

When you're dining in a restaurant or being served food anywhere else, don't dispense with basic health precautions no matter how good a dish looks or how expensive a restaurant you're in. Eat only recently cooked foods. Follow this rule: if it's not still hot, it was cooked too long ago. If you eat meat, make sure it is well done—especially fish and other seafood, for they are liable to carry diseases. Wipe any wet silverware or plates before use. If your drinking glass looks dirty, use your own mug. Drink only boiled or bottled drinks, or bring a jug of purified water to the restaurant with you. Avoid foods cooked in old grease, a common problem with fried food from street vendors.

If you have doubts about the cleanliness of a restaurant's fare, don't be afraid to wander into the kitchen. If it looks like a war zone, you may be wise to eat elsewhere, but if it looks fairly clean, the food will probably be the same. Ask other travelers about the best restaurants they've found. And use your guidebook's suggestions as well—but do so with caution. A mention in a guidebook means lots of business to a restaurant. In most cases, a restaurant puts on its best behavior after such a mention, but some restaurants—since the guidebook's blurb keeps a steady stream of travelers coming through its door—raise their prices while allowing the quality of food and service to deteriorate. Of course, a place praised by your guidebook may have changed since the book was written.

Etiquette

It is important to be aware of cultural norms that surround eating. Virtually all cultures have some do's and don'ts of eating etiquette. Study your particular guidebook to learn the customs of the area you'll be visiting.

In India's Gujarat state, Sue and I met a young Indian couple, who invited us to dinner. During our main course in the small, locals-only restaurant our friends had selected, the fiery Gujarati food began to heat up my sinuses. I leaned back from the table and emptied my runny nose lustily into a tissue I pulled from my pocket. Immediately the restaurant fell silent. The couple with whom we were dining halted in mid-bite. Everyone in the restaurant looked at me as if I were a leper. I should have been aware that nose blowing is considered especially offensive in India.

It's worth mentioning that in just about every Hindu and Muslim area of the world, it is correct to eat with only the right hand. It is considered rude to eat with the left hand, which traditionally has been used to clean the body after defecating. While that practice may or may not be common today in the area you'll be visiting, the custom of eating only with the right hand survives. While you may drink from a glass with your left hand, your best bet is to keep that hand in your lap, out of temptation's way. In fact, sitting on my left hand is the only tactic that works for me. In addition to using only the right hand for eating, you must also shake hands or touch someone only with your right hand.

In many places tipping is not expected. You should not leave a tip where none is expected, no matter how delicious your meal or how good your service. Likewise, if custom calls for a 5 percent tip, don't leave 20 percent. Tipping more than expected, or tipping when not customary, does two things. First, it reinforces the notion that Westerners are so rich that their money has no value to them. That notion provides justification to some unscrupulous locals who cheat Western visitors. Second, if enough Westerners leave unexpected tips, the practice will come to be expected of everyone, including locals who may not be able to afford a tip on top of the price of their meal.

Ch. 11
What to Bring

Travel light.

Anyone who has traveled much, backpacked much, or even moved across town knows the undeniable truth of that statement. Every travel guide worth mention admonishes its readers to jettison everything but the barest essentials before leaving home. How do you go about doing this—especially if you're preparing to take your first trip into the developing world's backcountry?

Will power.

To fight the desire to take a lot, two methods will help. First, make lists. Make lists of everything you plan to take—a toiletry list, a medical-kit list, a cook-kit list, a clothing list, and so on. Then sit down with all the lists spread out on the table before you. Go over each item in your mind, searching for unnecessary items.

Say you will have a lighter in an outer pocket for burning toilet paper and waterproof matches in your emergency kit. Do you really need the other lighter you have with your stove? Also, consider the amount of each item you plan to take. Do you really need 50 aspirin tablets? Won't 20 be enough? Can you photocopy only the parts of your guidebook you're going to need? And how many reading books do you need to start with? There are generally plenty available in English for trade or sale, no matter where you go.

Second, use the smallest pack you can imagine will do for your purpose. If you've got space, you'll fill it. If you don't, you'll agonize and then you'll do without. Your back will be happy. Anyone else who handles your luggage will be happy. You'll be happy.

Practice packing several days before you leave. That way you will have plenty of time to agonize—or to buy a bigger pack. When you practice-pack, don't worry much about where items should go in the pack. That is determined during the first few days of a trip. At the outset your main concern is with overall space. If you'll be camping without a group to provide your basic equipment, the first thing you'll pack will be your sleeping bag. Does it fill its stuff sack? Perhaps a smaller stuff sack will do. Every cubic inch you save will leave room for additional important things.

Other things to look for as you pack:

• *Pills that rattle in their bottle—that's excess space. Can you put one half-bottle's worth of pills in a marked plastic bag and add it to another half-full bottle?*

• *Your clothing will take up a lot of space. With it as much as with anything, you can always do with less. Think Gandhi.*

• *Consider your cook kit. Can you get along without those extra plates? Are you using metal utensils rather than unbreakable plastic?*

• *And for camera gear, it may be time to invest in that one-lens-does-it-all zoom you've had your eye on rather than carrying your usual wide-angle, telephoto and 50-mm lenses. You'll save weight plus the hassle of frequent lens changes.*

The main point is to consider everything as you put it in the pack. Can you make it smaller? Lighter? Can you discard it? Take it only if it's something you absolutely can't do without.

Suggested List for Group Members

Backpack or duffle bag	Alarm watch	Games/playing cards
Day pack	Camera/lens	Travel guidebooks
Water purifier	Film	Language book
Pad, self-inflating	Binoculars	Reading material
Clothing	Flashlight	Maps
Footwear	Candle	Laundry detergent
Scarf/bandana	Water bottle	Earplugs
Visor or brimmed hat	Food for snacking	Padlock
Sunglasses, strap	Knife	

Additional Items if Traveling Without Group Support

Sleeping bag	Cook kit, including:	Mug
Tent	Lighter	Plastic silverware
Stove	Pot	
Fuel container(s)	Lid/frying pan	
Food	Scrubber	

Writing Kit

Note pad	Envelopes, stamps
Pens	Postcards, aerograms
Address book	

Emergency Kit

Repair kit for self-inflating pad	Plastic bags
Rope	Zip-loc storage bags
Lighter or matches in waterproof container	Camera battery
Duct tape	Flashlight batteries, bulb
Stove repair kit	Iodine tablets
Sewing kit	

Passport Holder

Passport	Personal checks	Currency-stable
Vaccination card	Traveler's checks	Airline ticket
American Express card	Currency-local	Paper, pen

Toiletry Kit

Comb	Toothpaste	Towel
Deodorant	Dental floss	Feminine napkins or tampons
Toilet paper	Soap	Razor
Toothbrush	Shampoo	

Descriptions of Listed Items

Address book   For writing all those postcards to folks back home. Leave a copy of the book at home in case you lose it.

Airline ticket   Best to keep it with you in your passport holder at all times. Most are refundable these days, but getting a refund in the developing world can be a real chore.

Alarm watch   Crucial for all those buses, trains and planes you've got to hurry up and wait around for. Much better than a heavier, bulkier travel alarm clock.

American Express card   As discussed in Ch. 4, don't leave home without it. You can use your American Express card to get cash (in the form of traveler's checks) and mail, and you can use it to pay for flights, hotel rooms and meals. The large cities of the developing world are quickly entering the age of plastic money.

Backpack or duffle bag   See Ch. 12.

Binoculars   A personal favorite of mine. Unless you're a serious bird watcher, you probably won't use binoculars enough to justify carrying a larger pair, despite their superior optics. Some folks claim a good zoom lens is all the binoculars they need.

Camera/lens   See Ch. 4.

Camera battery   Most of today's cameras require tiny batteries. These batteries are impossible to find in the developing world, so find out what your camera needs, and carry an extra (or two, if that's what your camera requires), even if the ones in your camera are brand new.

Candle   For when the moon alone won't suffice, and the nearest electric line is far away. Candle lanterns are nice, but a candle alone should suffice, since ounces are vital.

Clothing   See Ch. 13.

Comb   A brush is heavier and bulkier.

Cook kit   If you'll be cooking on your trip, an aluminum cook kit is essential. Stainless steel kits are too heavy, although they're sturdier and more functional than aluminum kits.

Currency-local   Be sure you have plenty before you head for the hills, since places to change travelers' checks into local cash will be rare once you leave the big cities. Always carry as many small bills as you can, since guest-house and restaurant proprietors in the backcountry are often reluctant to break large bills. Dirty or torn bills are avoided by everyone in the developing world and you should avoid them too.

Currency-stable   Keep anywhere from one hundred to several hundred dollars of cash on you in any stable currency like American dollars, British pounds, French francs or German marks. Despite the wide acceptance of travelers' checks throughout the world, invariably there will come times when only cash will do—and only Western cash at that (see Ch. 4). Smaller bills are also effective as sweeteners to seal a tough bargaining session for a particular item you can't do without. Overall, the dollar is the money of choice. Next best is the currency of the European country that colonized the developing country you're visiting. British pounds are easy to change in Kenya, and German marks are popular in Tanzania. For Central and South America take dollars. Of course, cash is best if you're thinking about playing the black market anytime during your travels. But before you do, read Ch. 6.

Day pack   For day hikes and around-town jaunts. If you have a backpack that has a top compartment or an outside pocket that detaches and becomes a day pack, you're ahead of the game.

Dental floss   You'd have a hard time finding it in the developing world.

Deodorant   If you'll be doing much walking or hard riding, deodorant will be useless, but it goes a long way toward restoring spirits at the end of a long, sweaty day when no clean-up facilities are available. Bring just a little in a small container.

Duct tape   The bind-all, fix-all tape of choice for the traveling crowd. I once met a volunteer worker at the Arctic National Wildlife Refuge in Alaska whose pants were more tape than cloth. You probably won't have to go that far, but a few feet of the stuff will work wonders. Wrap it around a short pencil or pen to save space (then you'll also have an emergency writing implement).

Earplugs   The inexpensive foam variety snipped in half to be less conspicuous is essential to battle the many loud noises in the developing world.

Emergency kit   A nylon stuff sack about four inches wide by six inches deep should be big enough to hold everything. See the descriptions of the particular items.

Envelopes/stamps   If you're a letter writer, have a few of each handy.

Feminine napkins   Many women find that wearing these every day overseas makes washing their underwear an easy task. The light-day variety isn't too bulky.

Film   See Ch. 4.

Flashlight   Keep it small and light, but make sure it's reliable.

Flashlight batteries, bulb   Take a spare set.

Food   See Ch. 10.

Food for snacking   Since the restaurants or tea houses on the trail may be closed, crowded or too dirty to consider, always keep at least one meal's worth of snack food in your pack. It also comes in handy when your international flight is delayed.

Footwear   See Ch. 13.

Fuel container(s)   Since it is illegal to transport flammable liquids on an airplane flight, you'll be dependent on the fuels you can find in the developing world. (See Ch. 12 for fuel information.) Bring adequate containers for the fuel you'll need. Sigg and MSR metal fuel bottles work well.

Games/playing cards   A small magnetic backgammon board, a magnetic chess game or a deck of cards can help you survive a lengthy train ride or a long wait for a bus ticket.

Iodine tablets   As a back-up to your water purifier.

Knife   You'll use a multipurpose knife continuously on your trip. When buying one, look over its array of specialty blades and accoutrements carefully. I use the scissors on my knife often, although I never thought I would when I bought it. If you fish, you may want a fish-scaler blade.

Language book   No matter how little of the local language you use, if you use any at all you'll be treated with more respect. Spend a little time learning the language before you leave home. Purchase a language book or study the language chapter of a guidebook to the area you'll be visiting. The same language book or chapter is nice to have along on your journey too, if you can afford the weight.

Laundry detergent   Unless you're part of a group trip whose workers handle laundry, you'll be diving elbow-deep into tubs of water every few days to wash the few clothes you'll be carrying—unless you hire someone to do it. Either way, you'll need detergent. Don't bring much, however, as little packets of laundry detergent are available in even the smallest towns, no matter how far in the outback.

Lid/frying pan   To conserve fuel while heating liquids, it is important to have a snug-fitting pot lid. The lid will also work as a frying pan and an extra plate. Backpacker frying pans with nonstick surfaces are available but they're heavy. Still, if you do a lot of frying, one may be worth taking.

Lighter   A cheap disposable one works great. You'll use it to light your stove and candle, as a quickie source of light on its own, and to burn your toilet paper and other paper trash on the trail.

Lighter or matches in waterproof container   You'll need some sort of backup to your main lighter.

Maps   Generally, stores in the large city closest to the backcountry area you'll be visiting will carry maps of the area. Any maps available will make a good addition to the small maps that will be included in your guidebook. Be sure to learn to read a topographic map before you leave home.

Mug   The bigger the better. I use a plastic 16-ounce measuring cup. It's big enough for soup, oatmeal or stew, but small enough for a cup of coffee.

Note pad   For journal and letter writing.

Pad, self-inflating   Self-inflating sleeping pads aren't cheap, but a single night on one will convince you they're worth the price. A three-quarter-length pad should be adequate unless you'll be sleeping on snow. The pads are also great as seat pads for long train and bus rides. They're fairly light and they roll up small. Fold your pad in half lengthwise before rolling it up—it'll be a lot easier to store in your pack.

Padlock   Locking the zipper on your pack or duffle bag with a small padlock will deter thieves. Some hotels require you to supply your own room lock.

Paper/pen   Good to keep with you in your passport holder for noting ideas you may want to put in your journal or in letters later, and for jotting information like bus and train schedules, and costs of items you're thinking of buying.

Passport   You must keep it on your person under your clothing at all times. Nothing is more valuable to thieves than your passport, so keep it close to you and out of sight. Replacing a lost or stolen passport can be a real hassle.

Passport holder   Since you'll be wearing this under your clothes for your whole trip, it's an important piece of luggage. Select it with care. Be sure it's big enough to carry everything. Does it have a zipper pocket for change? Will you have to fold your already bulky wad of traveler's checks in half to get it to fit into the holder you're considering? Be sure the rope or string that will loop around your neck is both adjustable and comfortable. If you keep your holder tucked in your waistband against your stomach beneath your shirt— regardless how sweaty and uncomfortable that is—no thief will be able to steal it. Money belts work too, but they're difficult to get into in public and they don't hold as much.

Pens   Available overseas. Just bring a couple.

Personal checks   You'll need a few if you'll be using an American Express card to buy traveler's checks while overseas. (See Ch. 4 for details.) Keep your checks safely in your passport holder.

Plastic bags   Rather than a raincover for your whole backpack, use plastic bags for keeping your gear both organized and dry within your pack. Small- and medium-sized plastic bags have found their way to the developing world by the millions, so you'll have no trouble picking them up as you go. Bags large enough to hold your sleeping bag or tent are relatively rare; you may want to bring them.

Plastic silverware   The best eating utensils are made of unbreakable plastic. You can find them in outdoor equipment stores. Be sure the spoon handle is long enough to stir down to the bottom of your pot.

Postcards, aerograms   Postcards available in the developing world generally lack the quality of most North American postcards, but the scenes they depict are more than clear enough to leave the folks back home filled with envy, which is the main purpose of postcards anyway. Aerograms are simply unfolded envelopes already printed with the amount of postage needed to be delivered anywhere in the world. You write on the inside of the envelope, fold it up and drop it in a mailbox. In most countries, an aerogram is significantly cheaper to send than a traditional letter in an envelope. They're available at post offices and in some stores. For more information on mail, see Ch. 4.

Pot   Make sure it's big enough.

Razor   Disposables are the easiest. Rather than carrying shaving cream, you may choose to get along with soap. You'll have to carry only a couple of razors if you pay for shaves wherever they're available. A relaxing straight-edge shave is available in most of the developing world for 25–50 cents.

Reading material   Books in English are available in big cities and smaller tourist towns around the world, although selection is often limited. Especially popular are fiction and nonfiction books pertaining to the particular area. Anything about Gandhi is popular in India, for example. It's also easy to trade books with other travelers.

Repair kit for self-inflating pad   Self-inflating pads are great for sleeping and sitting on, but they are liable to leak. If you travel with a pad, be sure to take a pad repair kit too.

Rope   25–50 feet of nylon cord are invaluable. Be sure the kind you carry is sturdy enough for crossing any rivers. It will also suffice for a clothesline and for tying items onto your pack.

Scarf/bandana   Another item with myriad uses. It'll be great as a headband, as a hair cover, or hanging from the back of your cap as a neck cover in bright sunlight. It can also brighten up your evening wardrobe, it can act as a mouth-and-nose mask in a sandstorm, and corners of it can be cut off for use as emergency disposable filters when filling your fuel container.

Scrubber   A plastic or metal pot scrubber is nice to include with your cook kit.

Sewing kit   One or two thin needles, a few lengths of lightweight thread and a few replacement buttons should take care of your clothing. One or two heavy-duty needles and either carpet thread or fishing line will handle rips and delaminations in the rest of your gear.

Shampoo   Bring some of the concentrated variety in a small container that won't leak. Shampoo is widely available in the developing world, but it is expensive.

Sleeping bag   See Ch. 12.

Soap   You can save space by finding a substitute container for your bar soap that is smaller than the bulky square plastic soap containers for sale in variety stores. Bar soap is available everywhere.

Stove   See Ch. 12.

Stove-repair kit   If you'll be doing much of your own cooking, you'll need to maintain and possibly repair your stove. Many stove manufacturers put out kits that enable you to do both.

Sunglasses, strap   You'll be wearing them a lot, so be sure they're comfortable, and be sure they screen out ultraviolet rays, which cause eye damage and headaches. One of the many comfortable kinds of straps for hanging them from your neck will come in handy also.

Tampons   You can find them in the developing world, but only in large cities, where they're expensive and selection is generally limited. Bring your own.

Tent   See Ch. 12.

Toilet paper   Always keep plenty on hand. It's light, and if diarrhea hits, you'll need it. It is available everywhere—in widely varying degrees of quality.

Toiletry kit   A Zip-loc bag works well because it is transparent and it contains spills.

Toothbrush   A plastic 35-mm film container with a hole cut in its top makes a great case for the head of your toothbrush. Film containers are also great for carrying other items like spices, skin lotion and petroleum jelly.

Toothpaste   Available throughout the developing world. Start with a small travel tube.

Towel   A hand towel is all you need. It is small and lightweight, and it dries quickly. You'll be amazed at how dry it gets you—especially if you first use your hands to wipe excess water from your body. You can also use a corner of the towel as your washcloth. Wash it often.

Travel guidebooks   Carefully select which to take. Some guidebooks are great, but many are worthless. To get started, read Ch. 2 of this book. Also ask the advice of anyone you know who has been where you're going.

Traveler's checks   American Express traveler's checks are the most widely used and recognized. British Thomas Cook checks are adequate. You are usually charged one percent to buy traveler's checks. Some banks offer them free to their depositors, and the American Automobile Association offers its members free American Express traveler's checks. If you've been thinking of joining, now may be a good time. Leave a list of all your check numbers at home and keep careful track of them as you cash them. Doing so will make replacing them much easier in the event of loss or theft. See Ch. 4 for more information.

Vaccination card   Keep it with you in your passport holder at all times, keep a photocopy of it somewhere else in your gear in case your passport holder is stolen, and leave a copy of it at home too. Losing the original plus your copies could cause an abrupt end to your trip. See Ch. 4 for details on what vaccinations you'll need and where to get them.

Visor or brimmed hat   A visor works well for many travelers because it is lightweight and can be stuffed anywhere, yet it provides all the sun protection your face needs. If your hair is thinning, bring a brimmed hat that covers the top of your head too.

Water bottle   A one-liter capacity is probably enough unless you'll be in deserts. Bring a sturdy Lexan or Nalgene plastic bottle from home, as leakproof plastic bottles are few and far between in the developing world.

Water purifier   See Ch. 8.

Writing kit   You may want to keep your letters, postcards and other materials organized in one of the writing kits available in the travel luggage sections of outdoor equipment stores.

Zip-loc storage bags   These are impossible to find in the developing world, but are great to have along. Bring several. You'll use them over and over.

Ch. 12

Gearing Up

No matter what you carry on your trip to the developing world, you'll survive. But if you carry the right equipment, you'll do much more than that. You'll swing your pack to your back and stride comfortably down the trail while others complain of backaches and shoulder pains. You'll have the right stove for the fuel available wherever you go. You'll put up your tent quickly and easily while others hassle. And you'll sleep well, neither too hot nor too cold, in your sleeping bag.

In the previous chapter, a check-off packing list plus a paragraph's worth of description was sufficient for most of the things you may consider taking on your journey. However, four items—backpack, stove, tent and sleeping bag—require more explanation. (Since these four items are expensive, if your trip will be short, or if you don't plan to do much backpacking or camping afterward, making do with a piece of equipment you already own may be your most economically prudent choice.)

Backpacks

One of the ways I've suggested to help you pack as light as possible is to choose the smallest pack that meets your purposes. But how do you find out what size and type of pack you need? That will depend on what you plan to do on your trip and how you plan to travel.

The first decision you must make is whether you should

take a backpack at all. If you'll be going on a group journey for the duration of which your gear will be carried by pack animal, having your backpack with your gear in it strapped to an animal is not a good plan. Backpacks are expensive. The main thing you pay for is their design, which is specifically suited to being carried on your back. Strap one to the side of a yak, camel or horse, however, and it'll be coming apart at the seams within days; instead, your best option is to carry your gear in a strong duffle bag with carrying straps which encircle the bag for added strength. The bags are available at most outdoor equipment stores.

For duffle bags, space isn't as crucial a consideration as with packs, so go comfortably big. Backpacks are another matter. They range in size from small day packs at 1,000 cubic inches to massive expedition packs at 8,000 cubic inches. You'll be looking in the 3,000- to 5,000-cubic-inch range—at the higher end of that range if you'll be carrying camping gear, at the lower end if not. The size within that range that carries all your gear and feels comfortable to you will be the right choice for you.

Just about everyone agrees that while an external-frame pack is generally more comfortable when walking on wide, smooth trails, an internal-frame pack is the best choice for the international backpacker for several reasons. First, since the internal frame is an integral part of the pack, there are no protruding lengths of aluminum or nylon to get caught in airport conveyor belts, narrow train passages or jungle growth. Second, trails in the developing world may be steep, narrow and even treacherous. The snug fit of an internal-frame pack makes keeping your balance much easier in such environs—a real bonus when you're on a tattered swinging bridge high above a raging river. Third, an external-frame pack generally has pockets on the sides for miscellaneous items and a space at its base for attaching your sleeping bag. Those pockets are handy when hiking on trails close to home, but they're also easy pickings for thieves overseas, as is your sleeping bag. In contrast, the narrow, tunnel shape of a good internal-frame pack dispenses with side pockets. Your sleeping bag is stored in the base of the all-inclusive pack, away from thieves, sharp rocks and inclement weather.

At the store, take your time with every pack you try on. As you narrow down your choice, spend fifteen or twenty minutes walking around the store while wearing each pack. Shift it from side to side. Bend over. Take it off and put it back on. When you've made your decision, make sure an experienced employee fits the pack to you. Most internal-frame packs have aluminum stays which must be bent to conform to the shape of your back. Once they've been shaped correctly, the confusing array of straps and buckles on your pack must be adjusted to fit you. Ask plenty of questions as the salesperson makes the adjustments, then experiment with minor adjustments of your own. Good internal frame packs fit your body so closely that they must be adjusted differently when you're walking uphill than when you're walking down. Become comfortable with those adjustments before you leave on your journey, returning to the store for assistance if necessary.

Stoves

A wide variety of backpacking cook stoves are marketed these days. Most are more than adequate for use in North America. The field narrows quickly, however, when considering a stove for use overseas. The big problem with taking a cook stove overseas is that you cannot bring any fuel along with you, since flammable substances are prohibited on airplanes. That means you'll have to use what's there, and you'll have to be particular about the stove you bring.

Kerosene is the cooking fuel of choice in most of the developing world—dirty kerosene, watered-down kerosene, kerosene stored in rusty tin cans and empty peanut butter jars, but kerosene, nonetheless.

Thus, a kerosene-burning stove or a stove which burns multiple fuels including kerosene is your best option for use in the developing world. For years, two stoves—one of each type—have been the most popular for use overseas. The Optimus 00 is a small version of the basic kerosene stove you'll see throughout the developing world. A pump pressurizes the metal fuel tank at the stove's base. From the tank, fuel is fed up a tube to the burner assembly at the top of the stove. The 00 puts out a steady flame for hours and is so sturdy it will withstand just about any abuse you can heap upon it. On the minus side, at 27.6 ounces the 00 is heavy, and with its fuel tank and burner assembly all permanently attached and aligned vertically, it is bulky. Also, the 00 burns only kerosene, so it can't serve you as a white-gas-burning stove on trips close to home.

The other stove of choice has been the multiple-fuel-burning XG-K, produced by Mountain Safety Research. MSR first developed the XG-K for high-altitude use. The XG-K's metal fuel line does a preheating loop-the-loop through the stove's cooking flame so all fuel is vaporized before it reaches the tiny jet where it ignites. The result is an extremely efficient burning system which works well at all altitudes, including the rarified air of the Andes and the Himalayas. In addition, the preheating loop also vaporizes many of the impurities found in kerosene in the developing world, meaning fewer clogged jet openings for you to clean.

When MSR advertises the XG-K as a "multiple-fuel" stove, it means just that. The XG-K will burn just about any combustible liquid you run across, including regular gasoline and diesel fuel. It works well with white gas, and it even burns airplane fuel if nothing else is at hand. The XG-K is a good choice for other reasons as well. The stove weighs only 18.8 ounces and its burning apparatus is detachable from its fuel canister, making it easier to pack than the Optimus 00.

As more and more Westerners camp and backpack abroad, the outdoor equipment industry is offering more stoves designed for overseas use. Both *Backpacker* and *Outside* magazines generally keep abreast of the latest in backpacking stove designs. Check what they have to say and be sure to note the latest models offered by outdoor equipment stores before you make your final decision.

Tents

If you'll be buying a tent for your trip, consider two things as you begin your search: how many people your tent needs to hold, and where and how you plan to use it. Tent prices range from $19.99 to more than $400. There's no use in your buying a North Face VE-25 tent for more than $400 when a $19.99 K-Mart special will adequately serve your needs.

If you'll be traveling alone, there are several one-person tents on the market that may interest you. There are also several small two-person tents available that give you a lot more interior space for a little added weight. They're probably the better way to go when you're alone. If you'll be traveling with one other person, a small two-person tent is a good choice provided you buy one with a vestibule—a covered area at the front of the tent. Vestibules are a relatively new addition to tents, and they're one most people quickly find they cannot live without. Since they add covered space to your tent, they're great for keeping your backpack and other gear out of the rain. Since they have no floor, they're perfect for storing your muddy boots or for cooking (and spilling) meals.

As a two-person party, you may instead choose from among a range of larger two-person tents. A larger tent will give you more room to move around, and will enable you to keep more gear inside with you, but it will be quite a bit heavier than a smaller tent. If you'll be a member of a party of three or more, the size of tent or tents your group should carry will be determined by the make-up of the group. While you can save some weight by sleeping in a three- or four-person tent, most groups break up into pairs and use two-person tents.

Some things to look for when shopping for a tent:

• Rainfly—A rainfly is a separate nylon sheet that rests over your tent to form a double layer of nylon between you and the outside. Without a rainfly, the nylon of your tent won't actually leak, but moisture will bead up on the tent's outside walls. One brush against a wall and you're wet. With a rainfly, that moisture is kept one layer away from you so the interior walls of your tent stay dry.

• Poles—The poles are the most expensive part of any tent. Inexpensive tents have fiberglass poles. They are heavy and brittle, and come in long sections that may be hard to fit in your backpack. Most overseas travelers opt for aluminum poles, the most expensive of which will break down into 16-inch lengths. Aluminum poles are also far stronger and more flexible than fiberglass. Be sure the poles for any tent you buy are shock-corded together so you're not faced with attaching pole section A to pole section B as a rainstorm bears down on you.

• Floor—Be sure to use a ground cloth to protect your tent's floor from the tiny holes that result from a night on sticks, stones and stiff weeds. The popular space blankets sold for use in emergencies make ideal ground cloths.

• Ceiling—If you'll be traveling in warm climates, a ceiling made of no-see-um netting is a wonderful tent feature. On clear nights, your body heat rises through the netting while you lie, untouched by insects, looking up at the stars. On warm, rainy nights, heat rises through the netting to the fly, where it is carried away by air circulating between the tent and the fly. In colder climates, a solid nylon ceiling will trap heat in the tent to help keep you warm.

• Interior space—Tents are measured by square feet of floor space. Don't let the numbers fool you, however. If a tent you're considering has sloping walls near the floor rather than walls that leave the floor more nearly vertically before sloping toward the top, much of that advertised square footage will be unusable.

Sleeping Bags

Your big decision when shopping for a sleeping bag is whether to choose down fill or synthetic fill. Both have their pros and their cons. Down bags are lighter and more compactable than synthetic bags. On the other hand, a damp down bag won't keep you warm, but a damp synthetic bag will.

There is no clear-cut winner in the down-vs.-synthetic debate. Until only a few years ago, down was superior when compared to heavy, bulky synthetic bags. In recent years, however, scientists have created synthetic materials that come close to imitating down's lightness and compactability while retaining the ability to insulate when wet, and at a price that is generally less than a comparable down bag.

Since the down-vs.-synthetic choice is such a personal one, the best way to make up your mind may be to rent one of each on different occasions to see which you prefer. If you like your gear to be as compact as possible, you'll probably choose a down bag. If, however, you don't want to have to be careful about keeping your bag dry at all times, you may decide on synthetic.

Overbags are increasingly popular as add-on items to sleeping bags. The best are made with a waterproof, coated-nylon base and a breathable-yet-still-waterproof Gore-Tex top. They add 10–15 degrees to the comfort rating of your bag, enabling you to use a three-season bag for winter or high-altitude use. In addition, they help keep your bag dry—a plus on lengthy trips when you're using your bag nightly.

Inflatable, open-cell, foam-filled sleeping pads are also fairly new arrivals on the backpacking scene. The pads, made by Therm-a-Rest, are a superb investment for anyone who spends many nights sleeping on the ground. At $30 to $50 depending on the size you choose, they really are expensive, but the pads' insulating abilities are phenomenal and they're incredibly comfortable. If you do choose to take a Therm-a-Rest pad with you overseas, be sure to take a patch kit with you too. Try folding your pad in half lengthwise before rolling it up; it will deflate to a more compact size than any other sleeping pad on the market.

If you'll be camping in the tropics, one item you may wish to carry with you is a sheet. In many instances, that will be all you'll need. On cooler but still humid nights, sleeping in your sheet and using your sleeping bag as a blanket will be more comfortable than sleeping directly in your sleeping bag.

Ch. 13
Clothing and Footwear

Decisions concerning what clothing to bring on trips to the developing world's backcountry depend on two main considerations: versatility and weight. Since traveling light is so important to an enjoyable excursion, you should consider each piece of clothing carefully before putting it in your take-along pile. The best way to keep clothing weight down is to choose pieces of clothing that can be used for several functions. For example, wool button-up shirts are decent for city wear, and they make a nice light-sweater layer when hiking and camping. Cotton-polyester shorts are suitable for hiking in areas where shorts are acceptable trail attire for men, and they can double as swimming trunks.

Cool Weather

When planning a cold-weather wardrobe, be sure to incorporate the principles of layering for warmth. Rather than carrying one heavy coat for use when it's really cold plus sweaters and other items to wear when it's just chilly, use long underwear, shirts, sweaters and a vest or jacket topped by a waterproof shell for maximum warmth, and any combination of those to cope with a variety of lesser conditions. On a warm, rainy day, for example, you may wear only a long-underwear shirt and an outer shell. On a calm, chilly day, you may need a sweater, but not your shell.

Various synthetics play an important role in today's back-country clothing. Against your skin, cotton and wool long underwear have been replaced by synthetics like polypro-pylene. Rather than getting clammy against your skin when wet like cotton or itchy like wool, synthetic underwear actually transfers moisture away from your skin to the next layer of clothing you're wearing, keeping your skin dry and comfortable. It hand-washes easily and dries quickly. Syn-thetics are equally functional against your skin as sock liners, glove liners and hat liners.

Wool is often the preferred second layer, although here too synthetics—in this case nylon fleece jackets and, in extreme cold, pile pants—are giving wool some stiff competi-tion. Both wool and fleece retain some of their insulating abilities when wet. Wool gloves and wool socks are still the preferred second layer for your extremities. For your head, generally all you'll need is a wool balaclava—a hat that folds down to cover your chin and neck. For your hands, water-proof overmitts make a good outer layer.

For extra upper-body warmth, down or synthetic vests or jackets are used as another layer. The same synthetic fill materials that are competing with down sleeping bags are competing against down vests and jackets as well—and for the same reasons. They're nearly as light and compactable as down, and they retain some of their insulating abilities when wet. In most cases, a vest is all you'll need.

For years, unbreathable, coated nylon was the water-proof, windproof material of choice for outer-shell material. Then came Gore-Tex. Gore-Tex is actually a teflon layer lami-nated to breathable nylon. The teflon has holes so tiny that water droplets cannot get in, but large enough for body mois-ture in the form of water vapor to pass out of the shell. The result is a breathable, and thus comfortable, waterproof layer. Gore-Tex shells and pants are also expensive, as are the other waterproof-yet-breathable materials now being introduced. If money is much of a concern, you'll probably be better off sticking to affordable coated nylon—especially if you already own a coated-nylon jacket. Pants made of Gore-Tex may be a worthwhile investment if you'll be hiking in wet conditions. Your legs work much harder than your upper body while hiking, and hence give off a lot more moisture. Coated nylon pants do not allow that moisture to escape, while Gore-Tex pants do, even with rain pelting them from the outside.

Warm Weather

Choosing your clothing for warm weather is simpler than choosing it for cold. Essentially, you want to stick with comfortable, loose-fitting clothes. Cotton is the most comfortable fabric to wear in the heat, but cotton-poly blends are more wrinkle-free for city wear.

Button-up cotton shirts and blouses are far better than T-shirts. They're looser and more comfortable. And since they're nattier than T-shirts, you'll be hassled less at airports and border crossings, and you'll be treated better at banks and shops. In many large cities of the developing world, the only public bathrooms are in large Western-style hotels. To reach one, you must look like a hotel guest. A T-shirt probably wouldn't get you past the guard at the front door, but a nice button-up shirt or blouse might.

Loose drawstring slacks or skirts are far better than blue jeans for acceptance purposes as well as for comfort. In addition, you can hand-wash and hang-dry a lightweight skirt or pair of slacks overnight. If you hand-wash your blue jeans, you'll be lucky if they're dry by the time you're ready to return home.

In hot, sunny weather, a brimmed hat is a necessity. Many travelers opt for a baseball cap or a visor, which stows easily inside a backpack when not in use. In desert environs, long sleeves and long pants or a long skirt will protect your arms and legs from the sun and will slow your body's moisture loss. If you'll be traveling in the desert for long, you may prefer a hat with a brim that protects your ears and neck as well as your face, or you may substitute a handkerchief hanging from the back of your visor.

Footwear

On any trip good walking boots or shoes are a necessity. You'll be amazed at how much walking you'll do on your trip even if you do no backpacking at all. You may have to walk into a city from an outlying airport during a taxi-drivers' strike, or perhaps you'll have to walk across the no-man's-land from one country's border outpost to another's—a distance in some places of several miles. More likely, you'll be spending long days exploring teeming cities or long-forgotten ruins, or hiking in the backcountry.

As with your clothing, so with your footwear you want to do the most with the least. You'll be needing shoes or boots for walking and hiking, plus something to wear around camp. In addition, you'll need a pair of waterproof thongs to wear while showering, and you may want to bring running shoes, casual shoes or sandals for around town.

First, you should consider the boots or shoes you'll take with you for walking and hiking. If you'll be doing little hiking, you could conceivably get by with a pair of sturdy, low-cut walking shoes. In virtually all cases, however, you'll be better off using boots. In recent years a wide range of lightweight hiking boots has replaced the heavy leather boots of the 1970s. Danner makes a lightweight hiking boot with an all-leather upper and another that is part leather and part sturdy nylon upper. Both boots feature a built-in Gore-Tex sock and are guaranteed waterproof. Asolo offers a sturdy yet light-weight hiking boot called the Trail IIS, which is ideal for backpackers, plus several lighter-weight versions for hiking without much weight on your back, while Raichle, Vasque and several other companies also offer a variety of lightweight boots for every purpose.

If you'll be carrying your own gear, lean toward a boot like the Trail IIS at the heavier end of the lightweight-boot scale. A boot with breathable nylon sides like that offered by Danner and others would be ideal for warm-weather use. An all-leather boot is good in rough, rocky terrain. If you'll be doing some serious bushwhacking or mountain climbing in cold conditions, you may want to use the plastic hiking and mountaineering boots now on the market. The warm, waterproof mountaineering boots are a must on any serious expedition, though the more flexible hiking versions in plastic haven't caught on as quickly because they are bulky and stiff-soled. They're great for river crossings, though. All you must do is remove the boot's soft foam inner lining, then pull on the hard shell outer over a pair of neoprene socks. You'll have the most stable river-crossing shoe possible. After crossing, simply wipe out the hard shell with a cloth and replace the inner lining.

The best way to decide what will work for you is to make a nuisance of yourself at an outdoor equipment store. If possible, visit the store when it is least crowded—Monday and Tuesday mornings are best—and try on every boot you think you might be interested in, taking your time with each to judge its fit and listening closely to what the salesperson has to say. For the duration of your trip, you'll virtually be living in the pair you choose, so your choice is important. Buy them far enough in advance of your trip to break them in properly before you leave. If you've owned only the heavy leather type of hiking boots until now, you'll be pleasantly surprised at how easy today's lightweight boots are to break in. But just to be on the safe side, bring along blister pads.

Once you've made your boot selection, you'll be ready to decide what else to take with you in the way of footwear. Try to combine as many uses as you can. For instance, several companies make a plastic sandal with a comfortable, wide strap across the top of the foot rather than the uncomfortable between-the-toes approach of traditional thongs. The sandals are aimed at bicyclists, who often carry them on long rides, but they're terrific for overseas use. They work well as shower thongs. In addition, since they can be worn with socks while thongs cannot, and since they have a stiffer sole than soft-rubber thongs, the sandals are great for around-camp and around-town wear. Running shoes also work well in camp and for walking around cities, and they'll even double as trail shoes if your boots give you any trouble. They also serve as adequate river-crossing shoes. If you're really trying to go light, a pair of lightweight hiking boots plus a pair of the wide-strap plastic sandals will be adequate. A pair of running shoes are nice if you'll be fording any rivers or streams. They also add a nice in-between choice on long journeys, when boots and sandals may not cover all situations.

Suggested Clothing and Footwear List

Items to be carried in all conditions are listed first. Items for warm-weather use are listed separately, as are items for cold-weather use.

For trips in all conditions
3 pairs of underwear
1 bra (women)
1 pair lightweight cotton-poly pants
1 pair cotton-poly drawstring shorts (men)
1 swimsuit (women)
2 calf-length or longer cotton-poly skirts—one heavy, one light for cold weather, both light for warm (women)
3 button-up cotton-poly shirts or blouses (at least one with long sleeves)
1 button-up wool shirt
1 outer-shell rain/windjacket
1 pair lightweight hiking boots
1 pair plastic sandals
1 pair running shoes (if desired)

For warm weather
3 pairs of cotton-poly socks

For cold weather
3 pairs of polypropylene sock liners
2 pairs of wool socks
1 synthetic long-underwear shirt
1 pair synthetic long-underwear bottoms
1 pair rain/windpants
1 heavy sweater or pile jacket
1 down or synthetic vest or jacket
1 pair polypropylene glove liners
1 pair wool mittens
1 pair waterproof overmitts
1 wool balaclava

Suggested Reading List

Listed here are some books and guides you may wish to read as you contemplate, plan and undertake your trip to the developing world's backcountry. This list is no more than a jumping-off point, however, since there are hundreds of books available on these subjects at libraries, outdoor sporting goods stores and bookstores.

Travel Writing

To really get excited about visiting any exotic part of the world, you have only to read some of the writing of some of the superb travel writers of the last 100 years, from Mark Twain and Rudyard Kipling through Eric Newby and Graham Greene to V. S. Naipaul and Paul Theroux. To find the travel writers and writing styles that interest you, turn to your library and to Vol. 3 of the *Traveler's Reading Guides*. The guides are exhaustive references to travel writing and writers. Vols. 1 and 2 cover Europe and North America; Vol. 3 covers the rest of the world.

Simony, Maggy; editor. *Traveler's Reading Guides, Vol. 3*. Bayport, NY: Freelance Publications Ltd., 1984.

Travel Guides

In addition to the travel guides mentioned in Ch. 2, there are countless other guides available for you to read. To find them, start with *The Travel Book: A Guide to the Travel Guides*, by Jon O. Heise. Heise's book describes and evaluates hundreds of travel guides, enabling you to identify the guides that will benefit you most.

If you're interested in an adventure travel tour, you may wish to look at *The Adventure Vacation Catalog* and *Sobek's Travel Vacations* in addition to Mountain Travel's *The Adventurous Traveler's Guide*, which is mentioned in Ch. 2.

Heise, Jon O. *The Travel Book: A Guide to the Travel Guides.*
New York: R. R. Bowker Company, 1981.

LeBon, Leo. *The Adventurous Traveler's Guide.* New York:
Simon and Schuster, Inc., 1985.

LeBon, Leo. *Where Mountains Live: Twelve Great Treks of the
World.* New York: Aperture Foundation, Inc., 1987.

Sobek's Adventure Vacations. Philadelphia: Running Press, 1986.

The Adventure Vacation Catalog. New York: Simon and Schuster,
1984.

Travel Basics

There are as many advice and how-to guides on the vagaries of
travel as there are types of traveler and ways to travel. There are
books on city travel, ocean travel, budget travel, traveling with
children and even how-to guides for the disabled traveler. Peruse
the library and bookstore shelves to satisfy your particular needs.

Black, Meme. *Tramp Steamers: Budget Guide to Ocean Travel.*
Reading, Mass.: Addison-Wesley Publishing Company, 1981.

Fischer, Theodore. *Cheap/Smart Travel.* New York: M. Evans and
Company, Inc., 1987.

Grimes, Paul. *The New York Times Practical Traveler.* New York
Times Books, 1985.

Hecker, Helen. *Travel for the Disabled.* Portland, OR: Twin Peaks
Press, 1985.

Portnoy, Sanford and Joan. *How to Take Great Trips with Your
Kids.* Boston: The Harvard Common Press, 1983.

Backpacking/Camping Basics

A few of the best how-to guides to backpacking and camping
are listed below. Your own library and bookstore research will
reveal many more guides covering everything from winter camping and mountaineering to desert camping.

Doan, Marlyn. *Hiking Light.* Seattle: The Mountaineers, 1982.

Fletcher, Colin. *The Complete Walker III.* New York: Alfred A.
Knopf, Inc., 1984.

Hart, John. *Walking Softly in the Wilderness.* San Francisco:
Sierra Club Books, 1977.

Silverman, Goldie. *Backpacking with Babies and Small Children.*
Berkeley, CA: Wilderness Press, 1986.

Index